PLAIN SECRETS

Plain Secrets

An Outsider among the Amish

Joe Mackall

Beacon Press, *Boston*

Beacon Press
25 Beacon Street
Boston, Massachusetts 02108-2892
www.beacon.org

Beacon Press books
are published under the auspices of
the Unitarian Universalist Association of Congregations.

10 09 08 07   8 7 6 5 4 3 2 1

This book is printed on acid-free paper that meets the uncoated paper
ANSI/NISO specifications for permanence as revised in 1992.

Text design and composition by Susan E. Kelly
at Wilsted & Taylor Publishing Services

Library of Congress Control Number: 2007924329

For Dandi,
now and forever,
and in memory of Sarah

Nothing, I think, is more peculiarly characteristic . . . of American society . . . than its inability to see the Amish for what they are. Oh, it sees them, all right. It sees them as quaint, picturesque, old-fashioned, backward, unprogressive, strange, extreme, different, perhaps slightly subversive. And that "sight" is perfect blindness.

Wendell Berry
The Unsettling of America

CONTENTS

As a writer of nonfiction and the editor of a nonfiction literary magazine, I'm always disappointed, even a tad suspicious, when a writer changes the names of characters, because we all know that in nonfiction a character is a real, flesh-and-blood human being. So I am particularly disappointed that I have had to change some of the names in this book. I simply had to. The Swartzentruber Amish are a deeply private and insular group of people. Because the Shetlers have been kind, generous, and fearless enough to permit me access to their lives, I have vowed to honor my promise to them and change their names. I've also changed the names of the other Amish mentioned in the book, except for those who were unfortunate enough to have their names published in the newspaper and elsewhere because of buggy fatalities. I have also given pseudonyms to Jonas, his family, and the family he stayed with, the Gilberts. No other names have been changed. I have created no composite or conflated characters; nor have I changed a single other detail, line of dialogue, scene, or anything else.

INTRODUCTION

Feeling warm for the first time in over twelve hours, I take my place on a crowded wooden bench at a long stretch of tables covered with coffee and toast, jam and apple butter. I keep my eyes on my plate as much as possible, trying not to bring attention to myself or to cause my friend Samuel any unnecessary trouble. As a member of the Swartzentruber Amish, the most conservative of the world's Amish, Samuel has been granted special permission from his bishop in order to have me drive him and his four-year-old daughter from Ohio to Canada for his mother's funeral, and I do not want to illuminate my outsider status at this funeral meal by awkward gawking or unnecessary chatter.

The over two hundred Amish mourners and I are fed in shifts. About fifty people at a time sit down to eat bread and jelly and to drink coffee. Nearly a hundred of us, almost all Amish except for me, had talked and rubbed our hands together outside in the freezing north, waiting for our turn at the tables.

Once word spreads among the mourners that I have driven Samuel up to Canada, allowing him to bury his mother and return home in time to be at his wife's side when she gives birth,

Amish men begin approaching me, making conversation, asking how I know Samuel, making me feel welcome, at least for that day. The Amish women are polite but do not converse with me, and they keep their distance when the men are not around.

As I accept another piece of bread that I do not want but am afraid to refuse in case that would offend somebody, I begin to sense just how private and insular these Swartzentruber Amish are. Everybody at the funeral must understand that to have an "English" (non-Amish) person present at this sacred event has ever so slightly loosened the fabric of this tightly bound community.

The only person I make eye contact with is a small boy sitting directly across from me. He has curious eyes, as if he's studying me with the look of a bemused anthropologist. Like every other Amish boy seated around the table, my little anthropologist is dressed in a dark-blue jacket and pants with a collarless white shirt underneath. His hair is cut in a Dutch-boy style, with short bangs across his forehead and hair over his ears. His black felt hat and hundreds of others like it hang on every hook and nail on the four walls. In summer months boys and men wear wide-brimmed straw hats. Males of all generations wear hats with bands that are precisely five-eighths of an inch wide, the mark of a Swartzentruber Amish man. The boys' hats have brims that must be exactly three and a half inches wide, and to the untrained eye they are distinguishable from the men's hats only by their size. A trained eye can detect that the brims on the men's hats are wider by half an inch, and the hat brims of the ordained are a half inch wider than that. How the hundreds of men here today pick out their own hat and not somebody else's is just one more in a myriad of Amish mysteries.

People are polite, nodding greetings, offering me another slice of bread or milk for my coffee.

Rumbles of conversations in Pennsylvania Dutch punctuate the meal. Frost frames the windows.

Not far from me, down the table and on the young anthropologist's side, is a woman wearing a head covering clearly different from those of the other women. Her husband wears dark clothes, but not the garb of the Swartzentruber Amish. They don't seem to belong in the same way everybody else does. After the funeral I see them get in their van and head home. Later I learn they're Samuel's uncle and aunt, both of whom left the Swartzentruber Amish years before.

Not until a decade later will the curious boy and I meet again. Then I will learn the boy across from me was Samuel's nephew, Jonas, and I will know him as a young man who has created an aching chasm in his family, breaking his parents' hearts, risking eternity in hell, causing strife in his church, creating heartache all around, to which I am more than a mere witness.

But on this day ten years ago, I'm glad that somebody at this solemn gathering is looking my way, occasionally smiling shyly, letting me believe, if only for a second, that I'm not a dangerous outsider.

→ ←

I didn't know then that I was sitting at a funeral meal and literally breaking bread with the world's most conservative Amish. Like most people, I believed the Amish were the Amish and that was it. They rode in buggies pulled by horses; said no to electricity, no to cars, no to bright colors and TVs, no to war. In my naiveté I assumed they were preserving the heritage of America's agrarian ancestry and the traditions of a century ago, including sacred stewardship of the land, an unquestioning faith in God and his plan, a devotion to family that was somehow one part *Little House on the Prairie* and one part *The Waltons.*

In fact I stereotyped and romanticized the Amish, which is something millions of people still do. Mention the Amish to most folks and you will generally see a smile cross their faces as they recall the barn-raising scene in the 1985 movie *Witness,* directed by Peter Weir and starring Harrison Ford and Kelly McGillis. Ford plays an English detective hiding among "the plain people" to protect an Amish boy who is his star witness in a murder case. In one compellingly gorgeous scene, McGillis, naked to the waist, is washing and preparing for bed when she and Ford catch each other's reflection in a mirror. She turns to face him. The moment is bathed in a warm, soft, yellow glow as a thunderstorm charges the night.

Other Amish watchers in the know will speak of *rumspringa,* or the "running-around time." English love to gossip about the period of limbo when Amish sixteen-year-old boys and girls are permitted, even encouraged, to throw off the heavy restrictions of Amish life and enter the modern world until they decide to join or leave the church. Rumspringa, they say, is the time when all Amish kids go nuts: smoking dope, driving cars, having sex, ignoring their parents, generally partying their brains out.

The 2002 documentary *Devil's Playground,* an official selection of the Sundance Film Festival hailed as "haunting, provocative and unexpected" by the *Los Angeles Times,* features a photo on the cover of the DVD with a teenage Amish girl in the back-seat of a car, dressed in her Amish clothing and lighting a cigarette for the camera. The documentary opens with the sound of a horse and buggy clip-clopping down a country road, and then this iconic image of Amish life comes into the camera's view and it is established: Yes, these are the Amish—you know, the religious fanatics who wear plain clothes, hats and bonnets, who ride in buggies and don't use computers or drive cars. Not long after the buggy appears in the frame, these words, written in a baroque script, appear on the screen: "When Amish children turn sixteen, they begin a period known in Pennsylvania Dutch as rumspringa. They are released from Amish restrictions and can explore the 'english' [*sic*] world." The film follows four Amish teens through their running-around period. They have indiscriminate sex, use drugs, and drink like deranged college students on spring break; one even ends up selling crystal meth.

Although I'm not challenging the factual accuracy of this documentary—I'm sure the documentarians found four of the wildest, most modern Amish teens in LaGrange County, Indiana—the sensationalism astounds and the generalizations mislead. I'm sure that some of the more liberal Amish partake in this ritual at this level, but the vast majority do so on a much more subtle level, and some, particularly the Swartzentruber Amish, do not adhere to rumspringa at all. It is not encouraged or permitted. There are no cars parked behind Swartzentruber Amish barns. The Swartzentruber Amish I have lived among for sixteen years do not harvest corn during the day and sell crack at night.

Another view of the Amish could be referred to as the idealized chamber of commerce view. People who adhere to this un-questioning perspective see the Amish as somehow preserving what to most of us is a bygone era, a time before cars and com-puters, when America's families worked on their farms, a time when they cared for their neighbors and loved their country. If this view of the Amish were captured in an image, the image would be of a horse and buggy rolling down a country road lined with tall rows of corn, the sun beginning to set, reflecting just enough red light to see the smiling faces of the Amish chil-dren glancing out the back of the buggy, no doubt heading home to a haven of love and peace. These romanticizers of Amish life are nearly as dangerous as those seeking to sensa-tionalize it. These two opposing views of the Amish have more in common with each other than is apparent at first. They re-veal more about what outsiders *need to see* in the Amish than about who the Amish actually are. Thus, when some people look at the Amish, they see a dangerous and backward religious fanaticism that is about control, fire and brimstone, the heavy hand of patriarchy, and the subjugation of the individual, par-ticularly women. Others see a splinter of some idealized Amer-ica of a century ago, or at least a hint of a more recent past embodied in the back-to-the-land philosophy that mirrors the lost ideals of the 1960s.

David Weaver-Zercher writes about the "domestication" of the Amish in his book *The Amish in the American Imagination*. According to Weaver-Zercher, this phenomenon can be viewed through the lenses of "ideology" and "commodity." "To say that the Amish have functioned ideologically," Weaver-Zercher writes, "means that their domesticators have used them to ad-vance a given cause or give credence to particular ideas . . . outside observers have found the Amish to be wonderfully ambiguous (and conveniently silent) symbols and therefore well suited for being fashioned into vehicles of ideology." Weaver-Zercher sees the Amish used in this way when somebody appropriates them "to decry the perils of technological progress or highlight the need for land preservation." For loftier purposes, the Amish have also been used to "suggest what 'really matters' in life."

Another way we domesticate the Amish, according to Weaver-Zercher, is in our frequent "commodification" of them. "[This] process . . . demands two distinct parties: one that sells the Amish (merchant) and another that buys the Amish (the consumer)." Treating the Amish as a commodity, for example, can include depicting them in advertising or highlighting them as a tourist attraction.

Millions of tourists have descended on Holmes County, Ohio, which borders Ashland County and is, along with Wayne County, home to the largest Old Order Amish settlement in the world, to see Old Order Amish in their stores, where tourists can pay far more for an Amish rocking chair than what it's worth but still be able to feel good about their purchases because of the sturdy construction and fine craftsmanship. Chartered buses dump senior citizens off in Holmes County, or in Lancaster, Pennsylvania, so these visitors can recapture, at least for a sunny summer afternoon, a piece of America's mythologized past. Most of these tourists make no distinctions between different orders of Amish. They have come to see what they need to see, and then they leave. They now "know" the Amish, and they can go home and tell their friends all about them.

Even the different orders see what they need to see in each

other. The Old Order Amish look down on the Swartzentrubers, making fun of them for milking cows by hand and for taking baths only once a week. The higher-church Amish refer to the Swartzentrubers as *gruddel vullahs,* or "wooly lumps," for getting cows' milk in their beards. The Swartzentrubers, the most traditional of all Amish orders, believe the Old Order Amish, from whom they split in the early part of the twentieth century, have become too liberal and worldly, yoking themselves to the English in ways unpleasing to God.

As much as the Amish sometimes disagree among themselves, all, to varying degrees, adhere to the linchpins of their faith: obedience to their church and separation from the world. Beyond these tenets, to generalize about the Amish is to be a fool or worse. As Weaver-Zercher writes, "First, the Amish are not a monolithic cultural entity but are a diverse group of people, churches, and communities that embrace the name 'Amish.' Second, these various Amish cultures are not static entities but are constantly shifting and reformulating themselves. Third, Amish people, even those who live within the same church district, think and act in a variety of ways, sometimes in sharp contrast to one another."

I live in the midst of the largest Amish settlement in the world. Approximately forty thousand Amish live in the Holmes County/Wayne County vicinity, which also includes surrounding counties, the nearest being Ashland. When people hear that I live among the Amish of Ashland County, they get excited over having heard the word *Amish.* Usually the next thing they'll tell me is that they know somebody who knew some Amish guys who used electric chainsaws and drank beer at lunch, implying that the whole way of life is some kind of sham or at least a hotbed of hypocrisy.

But people truly in the know might ask if the Amish being generalized about are Beachy Amish, Swiss Amish, Nebraska Amish, Weaver Amish, New Order, Old Order, or Swartzentruber. Even within subgroups, different church districts often have different interpretations of the social template called the Ordnung, the rules of the church.

Within an hour by car from Samuel's farm in northern Ashland County, Amish use battery-powered lights on their buggies—buggies that have cool-looking faux-wood dashboards and heavy plastic windshields, like the kind seen in *Witness*. And not an hour by car in another direction, Amish farmers might use tractors around the barn, lease cars, or ride bikes. The Beachy Amish own and drive cars. The Old Order Amish of Lancaster County, Pennsylvania, have gas lights and indoor toilets in their homes, and might as well be English, according to some of their less modern brethren.

Tourists do not descend on the Swartzentruber Amish of Ashland County, although somebody passing by might stop at an Amish person's home to see what's good at the produce stand. Unlike the visitors to the Old Order Amish of surrounding counties, English will not be permitted to pay to have dinner at a Swartzentruber Amish person's home, where the lady of the house will explain the Amish ways and entertain ignorant and often offensive questions.

To be a Swartzentruber Amish means having black buggies with one or two kerosene lanterns and no windshield, no homes with central heating—gas or electric, and no couches or stuffed chairs. To be a Swartzentruber Amish is to have no indoor plumbing, no refrigerators or freezers, no continuous hot water, no tractors in the field or at the barn, no blinds on the windows, no wild rumspringa. Although their more liberal brethren have agreed to allow the slow-moving vehicle sign to be screwed to the backs of their buggies, the Swartzentruber Amish have steadfastly refused to use the sign despite being thrown in jail and enduring lawsuits in several states. The Swartzentruber Amish reject the sign, believing it to be too brightly colored and too "of the world." To them, accepting the slow-moving vehicle emblem would be akin to trusting in a symbol more than trusting in God to keep them safe.

To come upon a Swartzentruber Amish buggy at night is to spy the faint hint of a lantern's red light, as if your headlights have shone on a reflector stuck in somebody's front lawn; but as you get closer and if you're not going too ridiculously fast—although almost all of the corn-fed country boys in pickups around here do drive ridiculously fast—you'll catch what look like long silver splinters of something you can't identify, ostensibly floating independently of anything else, and this will be your signal that you've come upon a Swartzentruber buggy in the dark, where parents and five, seven, nine of their young children will be riding home from a long church Sunday of worship and socializing, perched on benches in the open night, belted to their seats by nothing more than their blankets and prayers, hoping you'll see them in time to stop or pass.

You will not see the Swartzentruber Amish of Ashland County on camera, unless it is against their will; nor will they pose for a picture or talk to a film crew about their ways. Although there are websites run by people who claim to have been Swartzentruber Amish, this is the first book that takes readers inside Swartzentruber Amish family life, and into the life of one family in particular.

Samuel and I first became friends without meaning to. I watched as Samuel, his wife, Mary, and their children moved into a nearby English house. As the Shetler family moved in, the accoutrements of being English moved out. I came home one day to find a toilet near the street and an outhouse being built. Electrical wires were cut and removed, pastel-colored wallpaper peeled off walls, linoleum stripped and discarded, carpet ripped off the floors. Soon shutters found their place next to a burn barrel or were stored somewhere to be used for some as yet unimagined need.

Every day that I passed the Shetler house, I would slow down, inspect how the de-Englishing of the house was progressing, and wave to Samuel, who never seemed to sit down. And Samuel's waves were not merely civil. They were downright exuberant, his arm bursting up into the air as if trying to capture a wayward balloon.

Not long after I began waving, I approached Samuel about boarding our daughter's quarter horse in his barn. Samuel needed a day or two to think about it. When I stopped by a couple of days later, he said it was okay with him if the contract he wrote up was okay with me. The only stipulation in the contract drawn up on a steno pad was a promise from me that I would not sue him if something happened to us while on the horse and that we'd be liable for any damage the horse caused to people or property. Later Samuel admitted that he only had us sign the contract because he had heard that the English sue each other over anything. His Amish do not sue.

About six months after we'd met, Samuel learned of the death of his beloved mother. For people without telephones or computers, the Swartzentruber Amish I know have an amazingly fast and efficient way of communicating. Although letters written back and forth and items in the *Budget*—a newspaper published in Sugarcreek, Ohio, that offers everything from news, front porch–style talk from relatives in other states, classifieds, word of births and deaths—are the main ways of keeping in touch, word of emergencies seems to travel by some unseen, mysterious familial and figurative fiber optics unique to the Amish.

The week Samuel learned of his mother's death at her home in Canada was the same week Mary was due to give birth to the couple's fifth child. Samuel had a choice to make. He could stay home to be with his wife for the delivery or he could travel to Canada to be with his father and other family members as they buried his mother. Samuel would be permitted to take the Greyhound bus to Canada, which generally took one day up and one day back, meaning that he'd probably miss the delivery. He didn't know what to do.

Although I didn't want to offend Samuel or be presumptuous because we had known each other such a short time, I volunteered to drive him to Ontario for the funeral and then back to Ohio. Samuel seemed interested in my offer and went to see his bishop, whose word on whether an English man could drive him up north would be final. By the time Samuel's bishop told him "go bury your mother," the funeral was only a day away. I figured if we drove through the night, we could make the funeral the next day and then drive home the same night. We'd be gone a total of thirty hours.

Samuel, his four-year-old daughter, Rebekah, and I left at about eight that night. The thought of a four-year-old child riding in my backseat for five hundred miles at night worried me. Perhaps it worried me because I remembered my own kids at four years old. It was then I learned that not all children are raised identically. The whole way up and back, Rebekah slept, and when she wasn't sleeping, she sat soundlessly in the backseat, heard only occasionally when answering her dad's Pennsylvania Dutch queries about her well-being and comfort. Samuel wanted Rebekah to come along because he wanted her to have some memory of her grandmother.

The hours passed quickly as we got to know each other.

Although I do not remember much specific dialogue from that drive, I do recall clearly one of Samuel's statements regarding his mother.

"At least she's not part of this sinful world anymore."

When we arrived early that March morning in front of Samuel's boyhood home, we parked beneath rural Canada's clear and star-heavy sky. The air was cold and the dark was quiet. My car's engine suddenly sounded unnatural, menacing even, so I turned it off. We both sat in silence for a minute. Rebekah lay asleep in the backseat.

I asked Samuel if he wanted me to come in or stay in the car. Without answering right away, he got out of the car and removed Rebekah from the backseat. Holding the half-asleep child in his arms, he looked at me and said, "I don't care what you do." He did not say this dismissively. He was exhausted and grieved, and he seemed to suggest that whether I came along or stayed behind, he'd be able to do what he needed to do.

I stayed in the car.

Later I spent the coldest hours of my life in the upstairs room of Samuel's brother's house, roiling around on the seat-cushion-thin mattress, praying that the heat from the wood-stove down below would eventually make its way up to me. It did not, at least not to the satisfaction of my face or feet.

The next morning I saw Samuel's mother in a coffin a neighbor had made out of slats of some seasoned oak he had lying around the barn. The coffin was nothing more than an old-fashioned, simple wooden box in the shape of a body, wider at the shoulders, narrower at the feet, adorned with nothing but an ended life, weighed down with loss. She was laid out in her living room, without formaldehyde or makeup, dressed in her Sunday best.

Not long after I woke up, and still several hours before I would sit down for a meal with the hundreds of mourners, Samuel told me that his uncle wanted me to ride along with him in his buggy for the funeral procession. The graveyard was on the land of a local farmer, just four miles away. The north-westerly wind tore through Ontario that day. Everybody huddled under blankets and pulled coat collars up over their heads. Seeing that I was about frozen, Samuel's uncle removed his scarf and handed it to me. A second later I had it wrapped around my grateful face.

When we arrived at the farm that morning—a four-mile ride that took nearly an hour—the fifty or so buggies in the procession found a place to park along the road or on the frozen grass of the graveyard. Prayers were said over the grave site as four young men lowered the coffin into the ground using ropes. As prayers and hymns were read in High German by the bishop in attendance, the four young men began refilling the grave. Occasionally the rough cadence of the High German prayers would overcome the noise of the dirt hitting the coffin. Every other prayer or so, four other men stepped in to relieve the men filling the grave.

From the morning of that funeral until today, my family and I have immersed ourselves in the lives of the Shetler family in the manner of few outsiders.

My own feelings about the Swartzentruber Amish are conflicted. I love and admire their connection to the land and devotion to family. I love the glow of the kerosene lamps at dusk and the sound of the buggies in the distance. I love their ability to say no to the latest technology. I wish my son and daughters had grown up knowing the small, manmade lake we live on as fully as the Amish I know are attuned to the soil, air, and rain. My kids have always been far more familiar with what's showing on which channel at what time than with how the lake looks when it swells with days of rain, or with the sound the ice makes as it slowly thaws and starts to crack at the beginning of spring. My kids have always been able to sing commercial jingles but have only a passing familiarity with reading the clouds in the sky or hearing the music the wind makes.

I also love the way the parents work on the farm and are almost always home, which is not something one can say about more liberal Amish orders who have chosen or been forced by economic realities to work in the English world rather than on the family farm. Hardly a day goes by when there's not a family breakfast, lunch, and dinner with all gathered around the table, the meal preceded by heads bowed in silence in what they call a "quiet grace."

At the same time I sometimes fear for the future of the children.

As the father of two daughters, I worry most about the lives of the Amish girls. A girl who has just finished her last year of school at fourteen will help her mother with her chores and her father with his until she gets married at twenty-one and has her own chores to do, her own eight or ten or twelve children to raise. Until she is twenty-one any money she makes will go to her parents. There will be no high school, no movies with her friends, no hanging out at the mall, no proms, no college, no career. But then I'll have moments when I wonder what's so great about hanging out at the mall as Madison Avenue turns our children into the next generation of our gluttonous consumer culture. And then I worry that perhaps one of these young girls would like to become an architect or a math professor or a doctor or lawyer and dress fashionably and look sexy, because as a human being she has every right to do just that, but that all this will be impossible if she stays a member of the Swartzentruber Amish.

And if she tries to leave the Amish, she will be entering twenty-first-century America, an America twisting in the uncertain winds of a global economy, and she will enter this new world with an eighth-grade education and skills prized only in the kitchen and on a farm.

And yet . . .

In my lowest moments—or perhaps my most honest—it's difficult not to bemoan everything we have lost in an age of a free market gone wild and imperialism run amok, with objectification of women the norm, and the violent hunger of twenty-first-century men haunting yet another era. As most of the world appears to be lost in poverty, genocide, war, and terror, I find it impossible not to be attracted to the Amish insistence on family and community, pacifism and peace.

I must admit that I have always found much about the Swartzentruber Amish way of life appealing and beautiful, perhaps even holy, and I have many of the same feelings about non-Amish life, our lives, despite all the evidence to the contrary. But I also choose not to turn my back on the parts of life I find disillusioning, even repellant.

More than anything, however, it is my relationship with one family that has helped me understand what it means to be a Swartzentruber Amish. The Shetlers, Samuel and Mary, and their children, Sarah, Rebekah, Barbara, Clara, Lena, Andy, Jacob, Mose, Esther, and the baby, David, have welcomed me and my family into their world.

Members of the Shetler family have become our friends, not just "our Amish friends." They have reinforced what I hope I'll never forget, which is that to have any real chance of knowing anything about people different from yourself, you must get to know the individuals of that social group, or race, or nationality. Nothing less will do. In our case it is this family. We have cried with them, laughed with them, worried with them and for them, shaken our heads in dismay at their behavior, and shaken our heads just as hard at our own.

I have gained access to this family because the Shetler family and mine have gone through much together. We were there when several of their children were born, and we were with them when their oldest child died. She was nine. We have eaten dinner at their house, and sought refuge with them when an ice storm cut off our electricity for three days. We've been there when an insurance company planned to seize their farm and when the county authorities threatened to throw Samuel and several of his Amish neighbors in jail.

I have wanted to write about this family since we first met, over a dozen years ago now. I've listened to Ashland County rednecks disparage the Amish, and I've talked with senior citizens who were selling Amish calendars filled with pictures of an idealized Amish life. And all the time I would have to ask myself, "Who are the people in the calendar? What does the guy behind the plow horses worry about in the middle of the night? And who is he anyway? What does the woman pictured removing a shirt from the clothesline do with the rest of her day? Who is she? What is her name? Is she happy?" I have tried to write not about all Amish people, but about a few real, honest-to-God human beings, as separate and unique as the rest of us like to believe ourselves to be.

Many fine scholarly books illuminate the differences among the Amish, especially the works of David Weaver-Zercher, Steven M. Nolt, the late John A. Hostetler and his student Donald B. Kraybill, now the preeminent scholar in Amish studies, as well as Kraybill's colleagues who have contributed to the series on Anabaptist studies published by the Johns Hopkins University Press. Hostetler, Kraybill, and other scholars have written indispensable and scrupulous books that merit close reading.

Still other books have been written as well, nonacademic books I call works of appropriation. In books like these a writer may write about leaving behind the world of fax machines and pagers and embarking on a quest of self-discovery while living for a while among "the plain people." Writers are usually escaping from something and into Amish country in these books, fleeing, for instance, contemporary professional lives or perceived environmental pollutants. Although I have found these books well written and enjoyable, the Amish often show up anecdotally, serving as backdrop to the writer's journey.

And then there are the books written by ex-Amish that are the most fun to read, for all the wrong reasons. One former Amish woman writes, apparently without guile or qualification, that "the Amish rarely smile or laugh." (When I read this quote to Samuel and Mary, they laughed.) Another ex-Amish, the son of an Old Order bishop who's now living an Evangelical Christian life in Iowa, wrote an alleged exposé in which he admits to committing incest with his sister (and blaming it on her because she touched his knee), having sex with cows, castrating cats, breaking the necks of numerous chickens, not for food but for fun, and brutally beating the horses of Amish boys and men on whom he sought revenge for perceived wrongs. On the back cover of his book appear the headline-like lines: SCANDAL ROCKS AMISH CLAN: MURDER, SEXUAL DEPRAVITY.

One can hear the grinding of axes in the distance.

It has taken me over a dozen years to gain the trust of the Shetler family—and to earn the access necessary to write this book. I'm still wondering why Samuel has been open to my writing a book. I know he likes and trusts me, but that can't be the whole answer. I'm certain he's well aware of the way the

Amish are generally viewed by the media. The Amish make the news only when there's an alleged exposé of sexual abuse, drug use, or perceived hypocrisy, or if the unfortunate few among them are killed in buggy accidents or, as happened more recently, a school shooting. Perhaps he believes that with my book at least the Amish will get fair treatment. However, because he lives in a black-and-white world, I fear he might not be comfortable with a story set down in gray.

When I sat down with Samuel as the head of the family to talk about how as a nonfiction writer I had to try to write the truth as I saw it, whether it flattered them or not, he seemed to understand, saying that nobody's going to believe something that's all good. I did promise to change their names, at Mary's insistence, but I have not altered anything else. As Samuel said when I spoke to him about perhaps changing the name of the county to protect his anonymity, "But isn't there a point when you change so many things that something that's supposed to be a true story isn't a true story anymore?"

Indeed.

And then there was the threat of "church trouble" to consider. Just last year, a full year after Samuel and Mary committed themselves to letting me write about them and their family, Samuel was named—in a mysterious and sacred ritual—one of only two ministers in his church; only the bishop outranks him. Now he has an even greater responsibility to his church and is considered a role model. In such a closed society, revealing the inner workings of that world is tantamount to a betrayal. Samuel has said that he trusts me to tell their story. "I know you'd never hurt us," he told me.

And I never would. Not intentionally, anyway.

The Shetlers are not a disillusioned family on the fringes of the Swartzentruber Amish. As a matter of fact, Samuel and Mary are highly respected members of their church district and are deeply committed to the Amish way of life. They believe it is a life pleasing to God. They believe it is their and their children's salvation. It is a life they love and believe they have chosen freely.

My goal in this book is to push beyond surface perceptions of the Amish. I have chosen instead to mine the raw material of their everyday lives in search of everyday truths. I am not an Amish scholar, nor am I a public relations professional. I am a writer who has found himself living among an amazing, fascinating, and flawed people. I choose not to sensationalize the actions of the most modern and liberal Amish and then generalize this behavior to all groups. Nor do I wish to mythologize their way of life, contributing to the sanctification of an entire group of people, convincing myself that their life is all about buggies clicking down country roads at dusk at a smell-the-roses pace, with peace and serenity filling every moment and everybody living in a utopian wonderland.

I have tried to tell the story of this Amish family with the famous conceit of historian Will Durant held firmly in the back of my mind:

"Civilization is a stream with banks. The stream is sometimes filled with blood from people killing, stealing, shouting and doing the things historians usually record; while on the banks, unnoticed, people build homes, make love, raise children, sing songs, write poetry and even whittle statues.

The story of civilization is the story of what happened on the banks."

This is a story about a Swartzentruber Amish family and their life on the banks of the stream.

And yes, occasionally the stream splashes ashore.

PLAIN SECRETS

ONE

Pop Cans and Doomed Pigs

On a sunny November morning more than a decade after his mother's funeral in Canada, Samuel ushers a doomed pig out to the silo corner, an innocuous-looking room attached to the bottom of the silo. He holds a section of board out in front of himself to wall off the escape route as he leads his victim to the killing room.

The pig turns around to poke at the board, trying to get past Samuel and back to its pen.

"He can't know what's going to happen to him," Samuel says. "But he saw his two brothers leave and not come back."

When they get to the killing room, Samuel traps the pig. He steps outside to load his .22 rifle. When he enters the room, he fires a single shot. But the pig doesn't die. When it drops, the pig kicks its legs as if it's running up a greased hill.

Samuel grabs the animal by its legs, spit style, and carries it out of the silo corner. He steps on one of the pig's hind legs and sticks a hunting knife in its throat, severing the jugular. The pig writhes in the dirt and under the sun of morning. It writhes more—writhes and shakes and bleeds; blood splatters the light-brown ground.

Seconds later the pig is dead.

Samuel doesn't appear to give the killing a nonpragmatic thought. He knows I live in a sanitized, packaged-bacon world. He gazes at me as if he's waiting for a reaction. I don't say a word, and I don't turn away. This is a working farm and a pig's a pig. I get it. But it's tough to ignore. Life one second. No life the next.

Hank the dog immediately starts licking up the spilled blood and then turns his tongue to the animal's snout and other parts in thirst or hunger or in some kind of primeval animal consolation. In the background Samuel's rifle leans against the red barn, its butt surrounded by brown weeds and white chicken feathers. Six kittens seek the shade given by the last leaves of a nearby ash tree.

Hank now wears pig's blood on his face like some ancient hunter who honors his prey by marking himself with the blood of his kill.

Ducks in a nearby pen quack incessantly.

To perhaps allow the dog to finish, Samuel lets eight horses out of their stalls. Five tons of horse stampede toward the gate that opens into the west pasture, devouring the space and time of the moment. Hank suddenly loses interest in the corpse and chases the horses, desiring antic exercise more than fresh blood. He barks all the while, snaps at horse hooves, dodges their kicks.

"He doesn't know when to quit," Samuel says, shaking his head at Hank.

Just after the horses run by, Rebekah, who a few years ago became the family's oldest child, comes out of the house with Esther, the youngest. Samuel tells Rebekah to leave Esther with him and go close the pasture gate.

Samuel pours two buckets of boiling water in a plastic tub,

puts the pig in, and begins to scald its hair. He then takes the animal out of the tub, lays it on an empty paper bag, and begins removing the hair with the same long hunting knife he used on the jugular.

At thirty-seven, Samuel remains thin and fit, a breathing, walking, working manifestation of utilitarianism. Physically, nothing about him is wasted; no part of his body is merely along for the ride. At five feet ten, 150 pounds, and not overly or overtly muscled, Samuel seems to possess not an ounce of fat, at least from what you can see. Only his wife knows the sight of anything other than his face, forearms, and feet. And even she may not. He has small, intelligent blue eyes that beam out beaconlike from the tanned face beneath his wide-brimmed straw hat and dark-blue clothing. Every step of this man conveys purpose.

Even the hair on his face, of course, serves a purpose. His reddish-brown beard has hugged and hidden much of Samuel's face since his baptism some twenty years ago. The beard is a symbol that he has been baptized and joined the church. Amish men eschew mustaches, which are linked with European soldiers and persecutors and associated with untrustworthiness.

Samuel is constantly in motion. Mary jokes that he does sit down three times a day: breakfast, lunch, and dinner. His day begins at four thirty every morning except Sunday, when he sleeps in until five. He feeds the horses and milks the cows before joining his family for breakfast at seven. Another Amish guy who lives up the road from Samuel has several teenage sons. Sometimes I see him sitting on his porch smoking his pipe in the middle of a weekday afternoon, confident that his sons are doing all the necessary work. Not so with Samuel, whose first five children were girls. Spying Samuel sitting down in the middle of the day would be as rare as spotting an ivory-billed woodpecker in East Cleveland.

At times I think Samuel's perpetual motion is an apt metaphor for the high mobility of the Amish. English often think of the Amish as being settled and constant, resistant to change and dedicated to staying put. In some ways this is true, of course, when it comes to adhering to traditional values and not being caught up in the latest technological innovation. Moving, however, seems to be in their blood. As a people the Amish fled from Zurich, Switzerland, to the Alsace region of France, as well as Germany and Eastern Europe, then to America—primarily Pennsylvania, and then Holmes, Wayne, and the surrounding counties in Ohio, and on to Indiana, Illinois and other points south, west, and north. Although the Swartzentrubers originated in Wayne County, Ohio, they now occupy over sixty-four districts in twelve states, including New York, Wisconsin, Missouri, Iowa, Kentucky, and Tennessee. Nearly six thousand reside where I do.

Harvey Shetler, Samuel's father, moved from Tennessee to Ontario, Canada, just after World War II. (Samuel's paternal grandfather, who left the Amish for a time, sailed to Paraguay before settling down in Tennessee and joining a less conservative sect.) Samuel grew up in Canada but he and Mary were wed in Ohio, where Mary and her family lived. After marrying, Mary and Samuel lived in Canada for a time before settling in Ohio. Since they've been here, two of Samuel's brothers have moved from Canada to Ohio, later settling in Iowa and Missouri, respectively, and his father, Harvey, joined Samuel here after his mother died.

To understand the movement and migration of the Amish, one must imagine a cell that divides, forming new cells, which in turn gather and cohere before dividing again, forming yet another microorganism, and other splits soon follow. A similar splitting of cells, leading to the creation of new social cells, has spread the Amish over much of America. They now have settlements in some twenty-eight states, with Ohio, Pennsylvania, and Indiana being home to nearly 70 percent of the country's Amish. Samuel often speaks of picking up and moving out west "for an adventure." Moving is in his blood as well as his people's. And move he does.

He is the quintessential Renaissance man. He's unassuming and capable. He operates an eighty-six-acre farm whose crops include green beans and yellow beans (less than half an acre); three different kinds of potatoes: yellow (not as starchy, first to be planted), red ("taters," planted at the end of April), and white (planted the first of June, popular for this area); two thousand onion plants; two acres of sweet corn; three hundred and fifty strawberry plants, and five hundred tomato plants. When he's not farming he's crafting wooden furniture, raising bees, or building a barn. When he needs to be, he's a mason, carpenter, well digger or duck raiser. The man can treat a horse's hoof like a university-trained vet, and he can birth a calf like a midwife. Samuel also has exceptional people skills, and an easily piqued sense of humor. Although he's lived in the area for less time than I have, he knows ten times as many people, Amish and English alike. He's intelligent and warm, curious about the modern world yet devoted to his own.

But as curious and intelligent as Samuel is, he—like the vast majority of the Swartzentruber Amish with whom I associate—

knows next to nothing about where his people came from. The fact that they do what they do is important—the historical reason for it is one more thing they do not have much use for. They are not a people who ask why they do something, but they are a people who do what they're asked.

Most of the Amish I live among have no real knowledge that their Anabaptist heritage can be traced back to sixteenth-century Europe, where young upstarts wanting change and radical reform at a faster pace than the glacial advance of the Protestant Reformation seemed to promise broke from the Catholic Church and the embryonic Protestant reformed churches to begin their own religious community, based to a large part on adult baptism, or "rebaptism," which is the word their critics preferred. ("Ana" comes from the Greek ava, meaning "again.") According to the Anabaptists of sixteenth-century Europe—as well as today's Anabaptists—only an adult could make the conscious decision to accept the gift of salvation.

Samuel can tell you that several thousand of his people were executed in Europe centuries ago, but he can't tell you that the persecution was brought on largely by the Anabaptist belief in this idea of a "believer's baptism," an idea that was considered heresy by Europe's established churches. Because these Anabaptists sought a separation of scripture and government, they were considered dangerous anarchists by established church authorities. These early Anabaptists desired to live by the New Testament, to live separate and independent of higher church authorities, to live lives of peace and nonresistance. They wanted to be the shepherd and the sheep. Samuel also does not know that the Anabaptists originated in Zurich in the early part of the sixteenth century just a few years after the Protestant Reformation began. The Amish, all Amish, are descendents of the Swiss Anabaptists who evaded persecution by Catholics and Protestants in sixteenth- and seventeenth-century Europe by fleeing primarily to France, Germany and later the state of Pennsylvania, and William Penn's promise of religious freedom in Penn's Woods. Although there are no Amish extant in Europe, they appear to be thriving in North America, particularly in the United States, where their population has doubled in the last twenty years. Now with settlements in twenty-eight states and Ontario, the Amish population is estimated at somewhere between 180 and 200,000.

Although all Anabaptists believed in excommunicating errant members, some also believed in shunning, an idea developed by Dutch Anabaptist Menno Simons, from whom the Mennonites take their name. Jacob Ammann, namesake of the Amish, borrowed the idea of shunning based on numerous biblical scriptures and tried to introduce it among the Swiss Anabaptists. Ammann's view of shunning and other issues provoked a division among the Swiss Anabaptists in 1693 that led to the formation of the Amish.

Just before the Civil War in this country, a group now called the Old Order Amish separated from the main group of Amish when the latter group sought a more liberal interpretation of Anabaptist life and joined the Mennonites. In 1913, the strain surrounding shunning showed again, and this time the branch that wanted an even more strict interpretation of the Meidung and more conservatism throughout the order split off and became the Swartzentruber Amish, a group that began in Wayne

County, Ohio, and took its name from two of its early leaders. (Amish Ohioans can trace their roots in the state back to the beginning of the nineteenth century, when Jonas Stutzman settled in the Holmes/Wayne County area after moving from Somerset, Pennsylvania.)

Although there are always new church districts and settlements cropping up among the Swartzentrubers—sometimes because of westward, and recently eastern and southern, migration; other times because of unsolvable disagreements over the interpretation of the Ordnung, or church rules, or because of the personality of a bishop, or a bulging settlement—there is still no sect of Amish more conservative or traditional than the Swartzentrubers.

Although he is not a student of his people's history, Samuel is convinced the Swartzentrubers, who make up only 5 percent of the world's Amish, have it right, although he would never claim to be saved. Many ex-Amish who remain Christians criticize the Amish for not being evangelical. The Swartzentruber Amish do not believe it is their job to convert the masses, nor do they assume they're saved, which would be prideful of them. They certainly hope they're saved, and believe they can improve their chances of salvation by living in obedience to church rules; but deciding whether they are or not is up to God and God alone, and they cannot presume to know for sure. As John A. Hostetler writes, "The Amish . . . [define] salvation as obedience to community as it is rooted in the Gospel accounts."

→←

Samuel has three more pigs to kill and skin. He's selling them, each about fifty pounds, for sixty dollars per pig plus ten dollars to remove the hair, without a doubt the toughest part of a tough job.

Two-year-old Esther slaps the pig with tiny hands in blue knit gloves. Her blond locks stick out from her black head covering, referred to as a cap by the Swartzentruber Amish around here. She looks at me, smiles, and laughs every time she slaps the corpse.

Hank has apparently tired of harassing the horses and has returned to the pig, which he guards from several feral cats attempting to get their fair share of the blood. Hank's a medium-size flaxen-haired mutt, clearly the best dog the family's ever had. And the Shetlers have been through a few dogs. A good Amish dog is one who barks at cars and strangers (at least at night), doesn't chase buggies or trucks down the road or spend too much time nipping at the hooves of plow horses, and doesn't bite or cause any trouble. One blue-eyed beauty was constantly nipping at the hooves of Samuel's horses and getting his legs squashed by wagon and buggy wheels. Samuel had to take him out in the woods and put him down with his .22. Another dog dug into the rat poison and had to be treated similarly. And yet another one had nothing that even remotely resembled a tail, which is something Samuel tried to, but ultimately could not, abide. "I have a hard time thinking a dog without a tail is really a dog." The tailless wonder disappeared as well. Hank seems to have everything it takes, tail and all.

In singsong Pennsylvania Dutch, Esther lets her father know she wants to hold up a pig leg and take off the hair, just like her dad. Over 75 percent of Swartzentruber men still work on their farms at a time when nearly 50 percent of more liberal Amish men work away from the home, and Swartzentruber children begin working at a young age. But at two and three years old, Esther and Mose tend to get in the way more than help out.

"Esther and Mose are my shadows," Samuel says. (When Mose began shadowing his mom instead of his dad, Mary referred to him as the "bedroom cat." Mose took offense at this name and returned to his dad.)

The water in the tub has turned a rusty color.

Esther babbles and claps when she sees the pig's tail sticking up out of the rusty water.

After Samuel kills another pig, Esther and older brother Mose walk over to the dead animal. Esther talks to the pig in single syllables: "Hey. Hey. Hey." Soon Mose, who moves like a walking brick with a pleasant disposition, steps on the pig's hoof with one foot and starts kicking the pig with his other foot. Esther mimics her brother. Samuel tells them to knock off the kicking, which they do for a couple of seconds. Esther returns to kicking at the pig's dead snout. The soles of her and Mose's black rubber boots are coated in fresh blood.

With the dog back in the field, several cats and kittens get their licks in.

Samuel's having a hard time removing the hair so he adds ashes to the water, to make the pig slippery and the hair easier to remove.

Esther asks her dad if the pig is a good pig or a bad pig. She decides for herself it's bad when Samuel takes it out of the water and flips it onto a paper bag. Esther tries to cover the pig's backside with part of the bag.

Samuel tells Mose to get Rebekah and Mary, who've promised to help scald the pigs.

"I finally figured out the best way to do the ears is with your hands," Samuel says as he tugs ear hair off with his fingers. "They're so floppy you just end up cutting them all up with the knife."

Amidst the splash of the pig being moved around in the water, the morning is filled with the sounds of occasional whinnies, quacks, moos, and crows.

"Hey, did you hear the joke about the rooster?" Samuel asks. "Why does he run around after his head's cut off?"

He waits a beat or two like any skilled comedian.

"He's not used to it."

Samuel laughs at his joke.

"I wouldn't want the lady these pigs are for watching me do this," Samuel says, throwing a hairless corpse onto a paper bag. An English woman has ordered four pigs for a cookout she's having and she plans to pick them up at noon, which is making Samuel rush the butchering a bit.

Samuel understands the way most English in America are disconnected from the food we eat. I can't imagine that the killing of these pigs is anywhere near as toxic and barbaric as what goes on in this country's meat-processing plants, but the butchering isn't pretty. Few of us know where we derive our food, unless we're talking about the grocery store. Most of what Samuel and his family eat has been grown or raised on their own farm. Samuel and Mary are pleased that their business is done locally, either on their farm or on the farms of close Amish neighbors. For their basic needs, they are in no way dependent on the state, national, or global economy. They consume little, and they produce what they need.

All this does not mean that they don't buy a few things they want at the Wal-Mart in Ashland or at the Dollar General in West Salem. Hitching posts can be found at the far end of the Wal-Mart parking lot. (One Wal-Mart in the area expanded its parking lot and erected thirty-seven hitching posts to accommodate its Amish customers.) It's not uncommon to see a Swartzentruber Amish man in a buggy with a large open bag of sour-cream-and-onion potato chips on his lap, having just left the Wal-Mart. The Amish I know best are nothing if not thrifty, and they tend to love the deals to be had at the Dollar General, which has been dubbed the "Amish store" by the English of the area.

Rebekah has finished with the horses and has come over to help her father with the pigs. I ask her if helping with the pigs is her favorite job. She knows I'm joking; she smiles and shakes her head no. What is her favorite job? "Dressing turkeys."

Much like her father, there appears to be nothing Rebekah will not do. The child loves a challenge. When she was ten she began plowing the field, taking her place behind five plow horses—preferring this to milking the cows, which began to bore her. She also helps with the machinery and construction. On any given afternoon, Rebekah might be helping her father grind feed or thrash wheat, or she might be hammering nails or mowing the grass with an old-fashioned blade-and-sweat-only mower. And according to Mary, Rebekah is also the best cook in the house, excepting her mother.

Samuel slits the jugular of another pig and walks away from it as it squirms in the bloodied dirt. He picks up a handful of chicken feathers, wipes off his bloody knife, and says, "Fine rag." He throws the fistful of feathers back on the ground.

After Samuel's finished scalding a pig, he places it in vats of cold water.

"That's as close to refrigeration as I'm going to get."

Rebekah, who is small for her age, pretty and graceful, walks over, sits on a roll of tar paper, and picks up a kitten.

Suddenly the killing and the play are interrupted by another of Samuel's daughters hollering something urgent from the porch.

"Mary's cut herself and she's bleeding," Samuel says as he runs toward the house.

Rebekah, Esther, and Mose stop what they're doing and wait for word of their mother.

Mary is a heavily freckled, big-boned woman who smiles easily. She has a pretty face and nice skin, and wears what the English would call John Lennon glasses. Her voice seems able to comfort toddler and plow horse alike. She always appears to be working—cooking breakfast, lunch, and dinner; canning; helping out with the produce—and yet she'll still apologize for the messiness of her house, even though the house is never dirty. At its worst, the kitchen might be cluttered with kid litter: some crumbs from cookies here, a bib or ball over there. Because she's constantly working around the house, there will often be boxes on the kitchen table being prepared to fill and sell at the Monday or Wednesday produce auction in Homerville. And there might also be jars of canned foods: apple butter, beets, honey, pickles, peppers. Her favorite outdoor job is shucking corn. She likes it because the whole family does it together. Family means everything to Mary, even beyond the regard that most Amish seem to hold for family life. She is deeply tied to her parents, who live only a few miles and a country road farther north. Mary's grandparents were among the original settlers of what the Swartzentrubers of this area refer to as the Lodi settlement, which started in the early 1950s. Originally from Fredericksburg in Wayne County, Ohio, Mary and her family moved northwest to Ashland County when she was a teenager. She's lived here ever since and hopes to stay here for the rest of her life. Whenever Samuel talks about moving out west, it's Mary's determination to stay near her family that keeps him dreaming from Ohio rather than moving to Iowa.

The slap of the wooden screen door reveals Samuel, who's walking back to the barn and the pigs while carrying two buckets of boiling water, which he pours into the plastic basin.

"Mary's okay," he says. "She cut her finger with a kitchen knife. But it stopped bleeding."

Now that he knows Mary's fine, Samuel gets back to the bloody mess on his hands.

"I'm going to try to do this one just right," he says as he lays the pig in water. He wants the water to be just this side of the boiling point this time.

Getting water is not always easy. The well is sixty-eight feet deep. A little gasoline engine is used to pump the water out of it. "I wish it was a diesel for safety reasons," Samuel says. "In the summer we were pumping twelve hours a day, six days a week, and we only ran it dry—or to where the pump couldn't get at it—once. We let it go for a while, not watering the garden, and then we were okay." The Swartzentruber Amish of this area are permitted small, stationary gasoline engines, as long as a belt is used to connect the engine to the feed grinder or the washing machine or the table saw.

"You have to move the pig around a lot too," he says. "It takes water and air to scald."

Samuel gives up on the last pig, a red one, and decides to use a small propane torch to burn off the rest of the hair. As he applies the torch, he tells Rebekah to hold a piece of plywood up to block the wind.

Esther and Mose bring out balls about the size of softballs. Mose's is green plastic and Esther's is a soft rubber. She comes up to me and throws me her ball. We play catch for a while.

A minute or so later a beater of a rusty van speeds down County Road 620 heading east. I have often thought about trying to get the township to erect a sign warning about the number of children here. Between the Shetler family and the Yoders just down the road, there are twenty-three children. Because there are no sidewalks, the Amish children have to walk to and from school in the road, and they often cluster in groups as they walk.

"Everybody drives too fast around here," I say.

"Did I tell you what happened to the girls the other day?" Samuel asks.

He tells me that Rebekah, Barbara, Clara, and Lena were walking east on County Road 620 on the way to their one-room schoolhouse, just over two miles from their home. On most days they talked and laughed their way to school, or they were silent and lost in thought as their metal lunch buckets stuffed with cheese sandwiches and fruit banged against their legs. Then a red pickup truck and a few rural English high school boys barged into their daily school walks.

At first the truck just passed them going too fast and too close, the boys shouting things the kids didn't understand and then laughing at their own idiocy. But then the pop cans started to fly. As the girls walked to and from school for the next few days, they had to watch out for the red pickup and the boys in it. The guys would drive by at sixty, seventy miles an hour and hurl pop cans at the feet of the girls. Full cans banged open when they hit the pavement, spraying cola everywhere, on the road, on the girl's capelike outer smocks. And then one day a pop can hit Clara in the temple.

The next time they saw the truck, the kids jotted down the first half of its license plate number, and the next day they recorded the rest. The girls had told Samuel and Mary about the truck and the cans, but the idea of getting the license plate number was their own. The day after the girls got the number, Samuel stopped by the office of the gated community near his farm and asked them to call the sheriff so he could report a crime.

The sheriff came out and took down the story, but Samuel said he did not want to press charges—he just wanted the violence and harassment to stop. Because there's a high school five miles down this same country road, the sheriff knew where to look first. That same day he waited in the senior parking lot behind a red pickup. When the kids came out he told them to find another route to school or he'd make sure they never drove the truck again. The truck hasn't been seen around here since.

"There are so many more people here than when we first came," Samuel says.

He's right about that. Since he and Mary moved to Ashland County in 1992, the population has increased by seven thousand, which does not sound like a lot until you factor in how many more vehicles are now on the road. But that's not the worst of it. Farmland is being bought up by developers and sold in five-acre parcels on which people build generic-looking houses, trying to pretend they live in suburbia, making the Amish feel more and more like they're being squeezed out.

A car pulls in the driveway. Samuel tells me it's the lady who ordered the pigs.

Samuel often dreams about moving to Iowa and settling near his older brother; he would not have to butcher pigs and turkeys, raise so many crops, or cut trees for extra money. His brother raises cattle and has a little furniture shop on his farm. He can let the cattle eat grass all year round, and then he sells the meat once a year. The rest of the time he works in his furniture shop. If Samuel moved to Iowa he would still farm, but he wouldn't have to raise bees, chicks, and ducks or work an orchard.

And there are fewer people in Iowa, and not as many pickup trucks. Maybe Iowa's a place where country boys wouldn't hurl pop cans at the heads of schoolkids.

The last thing the Shetler family needs is for something to befall another of their children.

TWO

The Leaving

For nearly six months after he learned of his nephew's leaving the Amish, Samuel said nothing to me about it. And then one evening as we rode in his buggy at dusk on our way home from a produce auction, with the sun as perfectly round and as bright red as I've ever seen it, Samuel told me.

"I ordinarily wouldn't want any English to know this, but there have been some strange things happening at his house," Samuel said of his brother-in-law's home, gazing ahead, over the back of his cantering buggy horse. "His oldest son, Jonas, left the Amish."

Samuel explained that he and his dad, Harvey, had tried to talk with Jonas, hoping that as uncle and grandfather they'd have a chance at changing his mind, telling him if he came back now all would be forgiven.

"He doesn't have any fear of God in him at all," Samuel said. "It's the first of my dad's children or grandchildren to leave."

I asked another question about Jonas that night, but Samuel quickly changed the subject, pointing out a troubling noise coming from one of the back buggy wheels.

"Loose bearings, probably," he said, as we passed fields of pumpkins.

→ ←

A few weeks after the buggy ride, I learned that Jonas had been living with an English family he'd come to know. When I called Nora, the matriarch of that family, and asked if I could talk to Jonas, she told me that she'd have to check me out first. I arrived at their country house five miles from my own, in an area that had been open farmland for hundreds of years and was now being parceled off and sold to families looking for a lot on which to build a ranch-style home.

Nora is a self-confessed magnet for strays of all kinds. She has three dogs, so many cats I can't bring myself to count them all, and six horses. She also has a young Amish boy fresh over the fence. When we'd been talking for five or ten minutes, a door banged shut and a short, thin young man came walking into the room wearing tight blue jeans and a sweatshirt advertising the benefits of beer. The young anthropologist I had last seen at his grandmother's funeral in Canada had moved to the States and grown up. And now he had moved out—and he hadn't just moved out of his home. He had left the Amish. He'd crossed over.

We shook hands, and Jonas said I'd either gained or lost weight since he'd last seen me, ten years ago. I told him that I was sure I'd lost weight, and that he looked a bit different too. Jonas sat down on a living room chair to my right and began playing with a couple of Nora's dogs. When I asked him how long he'd been thinking about leaving, he told me that the idea of leaving the Swartzentruber Amish first occurred to him when he was twelve. The gossip around his house at that time was that a teenager named John had just left the Amish, breaking the hearts of his parents and beginning his slow, steady descent to hell. About that same time, Jonas's father, Menno, told his son to do something, just a simple chore, a request or order depending on whether you're the parent or the child. But Jonas did not get to work right away, at least not as soon as his father had expected.

And that's when Menno said the words that planted the idea of leaving in the fecund soil of his son's budding imagination.

"Your name might as well be John," Menno said.

It was at that moment—and a not a minute before—that Jonas could picture himself as John, the boy who crossed over from Amish life to English life.

"Before my dad said that to me, I knew there were English out there in the world," Jonas said. "But I never really imagined somebody could leave the Amish and become English, not until that day."

A story Jonas overheard around the same time his father called him John also stoked the fires of his desire to leave. His father had been talking to another Amish man about the Bible and the end of time. The men were saying that at the end of time, people would have to pick a number. Both men feared they wouldn't be allowed to pick and they would starve to death waiting, forever unable to reach heaven. This conversation scared Jonas, keeping him up at night. He tried to open up to his father about being afraid of this end-time talk, but his father didn't go into it any further. Jonas wanted to leave so he wouldn't have to starve to death. Although Jonas understands that this story does not square in the least with any tenet of

Amish religious belief, it frightened him enough when he was a kid that the story has stuck in his psyche.

For the next six years, Jonas lived the life of a mostly obedient Amish teenager. He milked the cows, worked in the fields, went to school until the eighth grade, attended church, dressed Amish, honored his parents. But a closer look at the behavior of this young Amish boy would have revealed signs of discontent. One day Jonas happened upon a pitchfork that had been missing for some time and had been given up for lost until he found it buried beneath the hay in the loft. Not only did Jonas find the pitchfork, but he also located the perfect hiding place for the occasional cans of beer and the radio that promised to play country music day and night. The Swartzentruber Amish forbid both beer and radio. Eventually, hiding beers and radios was not enough, not for an eighteen-year-old eager to start a career in construction or as a farrier, wanting to live life as an English man instead of remaining an Amish boy. He had always dreamed of working construction, of driving bulldozers and backhoes. He even dreamed of one day starting up his own construction business.

When Samuel first heard that his nephew had left, he told me it had something to do with Kathleen, Nora's daughter, who is blond and pretty with a winning and open personality. She also had given Jonas lots of attention, which was not something the oldest of fourteen Amish children is likely to get at home. She had listened to his dreams, taken him shopping, taught him how to French kiss, and introduced him to the more commercial areas of English life. Jonas was wide-eyed the first time Kathleen took him to the McDonald's in Ashland, which features a black-and-white-checked 1950s diner theme complete with rock 'n' roll and movie icons on the wall. He had no idea who the musicians and film stars pictured were.

"Who's Elvis Presley anyway? Who's Marilyn Monroe?"

Although Jonas concedes he might have been infatuated with Kathleen early on, he insists they're only friends now. Kathleen, at twenty-six, is six years older than Jonas. She also has a two-year-old boy at home from a brief marriage.

The two got to know each other well around the time Kathleen started keeping her horses in another family's barn, right across the road from Jonas's family's place. Kathleen and Nora hired Jonas, then sixteen, to clean out the stalls. Soon it was apparent to Kathleen that Jonas just happened to clean out the stalls whenever she was there. Jonas would sit up in his room on cold winter nights, scouring the dark, waiting for the light to go on in the barn. I can imagine Jonas as an Amish Gatsby, searching the night for the barn glow, his own version of Daisy's green dock light. The light meant that Kathleen had come to care for her horses. Jonas would either sneak out of the house or make up an excuse to go to the stalls. It was on these nights in the stalls that Jonas began confiding in Kathleen, telling her how much he hated working at the sawmill, how he felt pressure to be baptized, and, ultimately, that he'd been thinking about leaving the Amish.

Nora related Jonas's story to me as it was told to her while Jonas sat in a chair not two feet away from us, playing with the family's dachshunds, not saying a word unless I asked him a question directly or he was asked for clarification. It was almost as if he believed she and I were speaking about somebody else, and I suppose in a way we were.

→ ←

The next time I saw Jonas, several months later, he was cleaning out the stalls and tending to the horses in Nora's barn. He appeared more confident and at ease in his new world than he had before. He wore a sleeveless T-shirt, blue jeans and cowboy boots, and country music played on the radio. He's a nicelooking young man with dark hair, wide eyes, and an easy smile that reveals slightly misshapen teeth. At five feet seven he is wiry, taut, as if about to spring. On this day his hair was cut close, crew-cut style. He hadn't been out of the life for twentyfour hours when he cut his hair, the bowl cut and bangs of his Amish identity falling to the floor, reduced to cultural jetsam. And he has a tattoo on his right bicep: barbed wire. He told me the tattoo is symbolic of his having crossed over, jumped the fence from Amish life to English. He offered me a hay bale to sit on while he worked and talked.

He made his first attempt to leave the Amish on an unseasonably warm Saturday afternoon in September 2004. By this day, Jonas had already spent six years thinking, fantasizing, and dreaming on and off about leaving the Amish and ending his separation from "the world." The timing was, in fact, fortuitous. His parents, Menno and Ann, had just left by bus to visit Ann's siblings in Canada. They'd be gone for two weeks, including two weekends. The first weekend was a church weekend. Every other week an entire Swartzentruber church group gathers in somebody's home for church. Amish reject having services in churches or in meetinghouses. They do not want church to be somewhere their people go only once a week. Because there should be no separation between church life and home life, the Amish worship in a neighbor's home. Sometimes called the "mobile sanctuary," Amish church services rotate among different homes, so that a family may be called on to host once or twice a year. So Jonas knew that if he didn't leave today, he'd have to attend church the next day, which he couldn't abide. What he did instead was post a note on his neighbor's barn, fearing that if he nailed the note to his own barn, his siblings would be blamed by his parents and other Amish for being complicit in his leaving. The note said simply that he was leaving the Amish. Nothing more, nothing less.

As Jonas talked, he worked. The Amish I know are nothing if not hardworking. He mucked out stalls, taking time to tend to the young Tennessee Walking Horse he'd bought and named Ashley. Jonas admitted to having affection for the name Ashley, claiming that nearly every girl he'd been interested in since leaving the Amish had been an Ashley. I admit I was expecting something different from Jonas. Perhaps my own preconceived ideas about refugee Amish—or about "rebellious youth" in general—led me to think a nineteen-year-old kid bent on emancipation would be trashing the life he'd fled, condemning it for its restrictive religion, its traditional ways, its insularity, its perceived sexism and smugness. Jonas didn't do this. He appeared to be embracing the English life far more than he was rejecting the Amish life. I expected the kid to be going a little crazy, partying like some of the Amish kids do during rumspringa. I didn't see or hear any of this from Jonas. Instead, he talked about his plans for showing his horse, maybe eventually breeding her, of taking classes to become a farrier, of getting a job working construction.

"I partied more when I was Amish than since I left. I saw

too many people leave just to party and then they come back and get baptized. I have nothing against living Amish. It just wasn't for me. I love my parents and my sisters and brothers. I miss being home with them at night and just laughing with my dad and telling jokes and having fun, but I just couldn't be Amish."

Jonas admitted he'd often partied with English and ex-Amish on weekends. He'd sneak out of his house, climbing down from his upstairs bedroom and running to the road, where he'd be picked up by friends. Sometimes he even borrowed English clothes and went into Cleveland, fifty miles away, to party. When he worked at an English guy's farm, he and an Amish girl were discovered riding a four-wheeler. The older he got and the closer he got to baptism, the more the desire to leave grew in him.

That first attempt to leave, however, was a bust. Jonas walked away from his home heading west to a hatchery run by an English family whose sons were often party partners of his. He had worked for this family in the past, so he figured the hatchery might be a good place to seek asylum. But Jonas did not get the reception he thought he would. The hatchery boys, around Jonas's age, said they didn't want him around if he was going to leave the Amish; they figured they might lose a lot of Amish business if it was believed they had helped him. They did offer to drive him home. By then it was getting late in the day, and Jonas could not face the prospect of a night without a roof. The kids dropped him off about a mile or so from his house. He'd been gone for just a few hours, not enough time to buy English clothes or even cut his hair; before he went home, he stopped by his neighbor's house and tore the note off the barn door before it could be found.

According to Jonas, almost all the kids who leave the Amish have a try at it a couple times before it's successful. These are mostly dry runs, when kids leave without enough cash, without a plan, without a place to live or a way to get there. It's as if they're priming their will, preparing their minds for a change in their destiny. Kids who leave the Amish are not going through some kind of maturation process, like English kids heading off to college. Chances are the church and their parents will come after them. They'll be told they're going to hell and taking their parents with them. Because the Amish see themselves as the shepherd and the flock, the community keeps an eye on its members. Jonas's leaving was never just about him. It affected everybody. This was why he put the note on his neighbor Levi's barn, ensuring that the entire community would know about his leaving, but without implicating his brothers and sisters. The Amish of Jonas's church district—like all Amish—have a duty to keep each other in line with the Ordnung, which are the church's rules agreed upon twice a year before communion. Although English might perceive this community watch as "ratting out" somebody or getting involved in somebody else's business, the Amish see this level of engagement in the lives of one another as helping to keep everybody close to the church and, therefore, to God. Even shunning a son or daughter is seen as an act of love. This "priesthood of believers" concept is a cornerstone of Anabaptist belief. They believe that as part of a community, they have a commitment to each other's salvation.

So after retrieving the note from the barn door, Jonas walked back home as if nothing had happened, as if he hadn't tried to end one life and begin another. He attended church the next day, just as he had every other Sunday for as long as he could remember. The week passed with Jonas doing his chores, taking care of his horse, and working at the local sawmill, but all the while the need to flee would not abate.

That Saturday night, six days after his failed attempt at freedom and two days before his parents were to return from Canada, Jonas lay in bed, unable to sleep, twisting and turning with the overpowering itch to leave. He decided he had to go. Early the next morning, Jonas got up before sunrise, and this time he left a note on the family's buggy. The note read: "This is Jonas. I left. I hope to see you soon, but I don't plan on coming back to stay."

After leaving the note on the buggy, Jonas went out behind the barn and just started walking. Jonas often went for walks on "in-between Sundays"—every other Sunday, when families do not attend church at the home of a neighbor but instead sleep in a little later, read from the Bible, talk among themselves, perhaps visit, or receive unannounced visits from, friends in the afternoon. No work is done except for chores. On this in-between Sunday, Jonas's brother asked if he could go along for a walk. Jonas told him that he wanted to walk alone, so he said good-bye and turned his back on his brother, heading out with no real destination except away. Dressed Amish-style, from his wide-brimmed straw hat to his bare feet, he made his way in the direction of West Salem—a little town where you'll still find black lawn jockeys, a town that's not much more than a few churches, and a gas station, bank, post office, and grocery store—five miles away. Not a cloud cluttered the sky.

Once Jonas got to West Salem, he stopped by the public phone booth in front of the BP station. From the pocket of his pants, he pulled out a piece of paper on which he'd written the name of an ex-Amish friend who had offered him a place to stay if he ever needed one. When Jonas called, the guy told him he had moved in with his girlfriend and didn't think his new living arrangements could accommodate an Amish kid on the run.

After he hung up the phone, Jonas heard the sound of car engines in the distance. West Salem's dubious claim to fame is a racetrack that draws car-crazy kids from all over the state. Jonas had always been interested in all things with loud engines and raw power. For as long as he could remember he loved watching English construction crews with their backhoes, bulldozers, and dump trucks. The sheer loud energy of these machines stirred his imagination. As much as he loved horses, the rough strength of the internal combustion engine was hard to beat. He sat in the sunny stands at Dragway 42 for a couple of hours, alone, watching the banged-up beaters race around an oblong track—starting nowhere, going nowhere—and listening to the noise of the straining engines and the sounds of the Sunday-afternoon crowd. He wished he were driving one of the cars. One day he wanted a car or a pickup truck of his own.

A full ten months after the day at Dragway 42, as we talked amidst the horses and hay, Jonas was still dreaming of owning his own pickup. He and Kathleen had talked about his assuming the payments on her truck when she bought another car. In his weak moments, Jonas often wonders if he would have left the Amish if he'd known all he would have to endure, how hard it would be making it in the world with only an eighth-grade education, how many obstacles he would have to overcome and how far he still had to go.

Everything was fine while the cars raced and the crowd cheered, but then the race ended, spectators began leaving and the sun started setting, just enough to remind him of the coming night. Soon, words raced around his head, making loop after loop. All he could think was that he had "nowhere to go, nowhere to live, nowhere to go, nowhere to live."

One of Jonas's friends had left the Amish the month before, so he considered heading over to his new place. The kid was living a few miles away with several other ex-Amish. Maybe there would be room there. Because Jonas had planned only so far as his leaving, he had no idea what to do next. So with the empty racetrack at his back, he started walking again. He walked for three miles and still had another ten in front of him.

"Hey, Amish," he heard somebody holler from a car as he was passing back through the town of West Salem.

Jonas turned to discover the driver was Noah, an ex-Amish guy just a couple of years older than himself.

He asked Jonas where he was headed. Jonas told him he had left the Amish.

Noah offered to call another ex-Amish man, who, at thirty years old, had been out of the Amish life for nearly a decade. Since leaving the Amish ten years ago, Dan Miller had started a successful construction company and owned a house that was often filled with Amish boys who had just crossed over. Miller told them they didn't need to pay rent for the first three months, hoping by then they would find work and have a little money. Jonas heard that a great many of the ex-Amish living with Miller were eating him out of house and home.

When Noah got off the phone, he told Jonas that Miller said he didn't have any room right now. Later Jonas would tell me that he believed Noah had not called Miller at all, but that he himself was taking advantage of the man's hospitality and was afraid he'd be asked to leave if Jonas were to move in.

→ ←

Using Noah's cell phone, Jonas called the Gilbert family. Nora and Kathleen had known Jonas most of his life, having lived down the road from his parents for over a decade.

"I've left the Amish," Jonas told Kathleen when she answered the phone.

Kathleen invited Jonas over, and Noah agreed to drive him there.

For the next few hours, Nora, Kathleen, Jonas, and Noah talked, trying to figure out where Jonas would live and work, how he would survive if he really crossed over. Nora, middle-aged and a mother and grandmother herself, told Jonas that he ought to go home. She didn't like the fact that he had left while his parents were away. She thought he had to face them and tell them his intentions.

When they left Nora and Kathleen's place, Noah and Jonas drove to a party some English kids were throwing. While at the party, Jonas couldn't help thinking about how many would-be ex-Amish ended up living from party to party, screwing up their chance of crossing over. Kids his age would leave home, drink and party, blow their money, and overstay their welcome. Then with no money, no job, no place to live, they would decide that all they could do in the English world was party, so these Amish would return home, get baptized, marry, and remain Amish. Jonas often wished the Swartzentruber Amish engaged in rumspringa, the running-around time, the way more liberal or modern Amish people did; but he admits that even rumspringa could not have freed him from his desire to escape.

By nine that night, Jonas and Noah had tired of the party. As they drove around, Noah talked to Jonas about making sure he had enough money to really leave at this time. One hundred dollars was nowhere near enough to leave on, let alone live on. Noah also told him that many ex-Amish, himself included, had left several times only to go back, but that eventually, with enough money and a practical plan, they were able to leave for good.

Jonas either saw the wisdom of Noah's words or was too tired, frightened, or full of despair to continue his escape. He asked Noah to drop him off a little ways from his house, and he walked home, back into the fold, again.

He had been gone from Amish life for a whole ten hours and was still in his Amish clothes.

Trying to sneak back into his house without being noticed, Jonas started to hear his dogs barking. The barks roused his grandfather, who must have been told about Jonas's leaving. His grandfather appeared at the front door, opened it, and looked around. Jonas crouched out of sight in a field speckled with firefly light until his grandfather went back inside the house. After a few minutes Jonas crept to the front door only to find it locked. And then he knew what had happened. His grandfather had locked him out of the house.

With nowhere else to go, Jonas went to the barn and laid his head on some loose hay. Soon his dog, Selby, a red terrier-and-beagle mix, joined him. Tired and defeated, Jonas fell asleep.

The next morning, the sound of chattering children woke Selby, whose bark awakened Jonas. His siblings, realizing Jonas had been locked out of the house and thinking he must be in the barn, ran out to find him. And warn him. They told Jonas that their neighbor Levi was coming over to talk to Jonas's oldest siblings.

Before they finished talking, they heard a noise outside the barn.

Knowing it was Levi, Jonas snuck into a stall, crouched down low among the horseflies and cow manure, and kept out of sight. He strained to hear what Levi was saying. Levi immediately wanted to know whether Jonas had "took his hair cut." One of the first things most ex-Amish do is cut their hair, which is as much a symbol of leaving the Amish as a beard is of staying. Levi, a furniture maker, middle-aged and chunky with red hair and beard, informed the kids that he was going to the sawmill where Jonas worked to tell them he would not be coming in that day.

I believed Jonas's story about Levi because I knew of the tension that had existed for years between Levi and Jonas's father, Menno. Menno had bought his farm first and then Levi built his house on land next door. The church then came to Menno and essentially forced him to allow Levi's driveway to cross Menno's land. Grudgingly, Menno agreed. Since then a certain friction has existed between the families, with Levi always seeming to get the upper hand. I've had my own moments with Levi, which have reinforced the fact that just because Amish men dress and believe alike does not mean they are all the same. Frankly, I don't like Levi. I don't find him particularly nice or kind or smart. Samuel is all of these and more.

Jonas had his own problems with Levi. He felt the man was constantly watching him, hoping he'd do something that would reflect poorly on Jonas's father, whom he'd already approached once with gossip about Jonas. "He came up to my dad and said that I was up at the barn [with Kathleen] a lot. He figured I'd get in trouble for it. When Levi got done telling my dad all that stuff, I said, 'I hope you remember that you have kids growing up and the same thing's going to happen to them.' His head hung low, and that's all I wanted to see from him." Furious with Levi and deciding to move back home before his parents returned from their trip, Jonas hitched up his horse to the family buggy and went to work. When he got to the sawmill, it was clear everybody there had heard of his attempt to leave. At first nobody talked to him. After a few days, everybody loosened up and things at the mill returned to normal. Nobody talked about Jonas's leaving. Nobody even mentioned it for a month.

And then one day while he was sawing a log, Jonas's boss stopped, cut off the saw, and said, "I couldn't believe it when you showed up for work that day."

"Sometimes people talk too soon," Jonas said.

Jonas continued working at the sawmill full time, making nearly $1,300 a month, all of which he had to turn over to his parents. No one said anything about the occasional tips he earned.

Jonas related all of this while he mucked out horse stalls and put down fresh hay, as if what he'd been through was the most natural thing in the world: a neighbor turning him in, sleeping in his barn, wandering around without a destination, unable to leave, unable to stay.

→ ←

The summer or early fall is the best time to leave, and that's when most Amish kids try it, Jonas told me as he brushed Ashley down. Anybody who leaves in the winter has to have decent money and a place to live right away. Wanting to shed their Amish garb, kids who flee in winter will need clothes for the cold, and will not be able to wander around barefoot in Amish clothes the way Jonas did on his second attempt at escape. Young men and women in their late teens will begin to be asked about being baptized in late September, early October. Jonas said he was being "hounded" about his baptism, everybody telling him it was about time to begin preparing for baptism and then get baptized, join the church officially, grow his beard, find a wife. Jonas dreaded baptism; he wanted nothing to do with reciting his commitment to renounce the devil, the world, and his own flesh, committing himself to Christ, and submitting to and obeying the Ordnung. He did not want to be Amish for life, or receive the Holy Kiss on the lips from his bishop. (Romans 16:16: "Salute one another with an holy kiss. The churches of Christ salute you." Women who are baptized receive the kiss from the bishop's wife. When I asked Samuel about the kiss, he said, "It's real quick.") As a kid Jonas had often been in trouble with the church. "I'd always get it for smiling at church or for smoking a cigarette." And then two weeks before he was to begin his classes, Jonas trimmed the whiskers on his face. "A lot of boys wanted to get baptized but they didn't want a beard," Jonas said. Jonas claimed he trimmed his fledgling beard because he didn't like the way it looked or felt. Elders at church noticed Jonas's smooth face and expressed their disapproval, telling Jonas that maybe he wasn't ready for baptism, which is exactly what Jonas had hoped they'd say. In most "higher churches," Amish men won't grow beards until after they're married, the beard being the symbol of marriage the way the ring is a customary sign of marriage in mainstream American culture. With the Swartzentruber Amish, willingness to let a beard come in during the time leading up to baptism is a symbol of a boy's desire to become an Amish man in good standing. For the Swartzentruber man, an untrimmed beard is a sacred symbol that he has been baptized and has willingly accepted the holy burden of being Amish in the modern world.

Complicating things for Jonas—as well as other young Swartzentrubers who want to leave the Amish—is the fact that despite or because of their extreme traditionalism and conservatism, the Swartzentruber Amish retain nearly 90 percent of their children. Perhaps oddly, the New Order, a far more liberal sect, retains not even six of ten. The cultural chasm separating Swartzentruber life and modern English life is a wider and more perilous leap than that for any other order.

⇥ ⇤

Four months after Jonas's two failed attempts at leaving, his big day came: January 14, 2005. This time he had a plan and some money. Again, his parents were not at home, but were scheduled to return later that night. Jonas had called Noah, the ex-Amish guy who drove him around the last time he tried to leave, and Noah had agreed to pick him up at the house of an English woman across the street from Jonas's place. All he needed to do was run across the road, use the English woman's phone to call Noah, and wait for him to show up.

"The night before, I went to bed, and I just couldn't sleep. I was just thinking, 'I can't believe I'll be out of here. I'll be English. I can use power tools and drive a car.' The next night my parents weren't home. I was going to leave the note in my bedroom, but I wanted it so everyone could see it. So I put in on the stairway. I left a note that said I was leaving and that it wasn't anything they did, but I found out that Amish life was not for me. I grabbed my birth certificate and my money, and I left."

A snowstorm had hit Northeast Ohio that night, and Jonas worried that maybe Noah wouldn't be able to make the drive to pick him up, but he left anyway. When he got to his English neighbor's place across the street, he asked her if he could use her phone. The neighbor had permitted Jonas to do this in the past, when he wanted to call ex-Amish or English friends to pick him up for a night of partying. He made the call and Noah told him he was on his way. All he needed to do now was to wait for his ride and hope his parents didn't come home before he could leave. His neighbor offered him soup, but he was too nervous to eat.

"There was a knock on the door," Jonas said, closing Ashley's stall door. "I thought it was my dad, and I thought 'Shoot, he found my note already.' But it was Noah. Then Noah sat down and ate soup and talked. It was snowing and blowing outside. I was getting nervous and I wanted to leave."

Noah finished his soup and the two of them left.

Soon, Jonas would discover that crossing over involved more than changing clothes and leaving home. He would find out just how much there was to understand outside of a closed Swartzentruber Amish life, and learn how many of his ideas about what it took to make it in the English world would be tested. He would feel just how powerful and far-reaching the tentacles of the church really were, realize just how few resources he possessed to make it in the outside world, and understand that his parents would have to choose between their son and their church.

When Jonas left that night, he had no idea the hardship and pain he'd have to endure—and inflict—in the months to come.

THREE

Remembering Sarah

On this warm, sunny autumn afternoon, almost five years to the day after the Shetlers' oldest child, Sarah, died, upwards of a thousand pumpkins cover the lawn. When I walk to the wagon, I see Esther and Mose standing in the back of it handing pumpkins to their oldest sibling, Rebekah, and their fifteen-year-old neighbor, Daniel. When Esther spots the can of cheddar potato chips I'm bearing as a gift, her work stops and she reaches her arms out to me, or rather, to the chips. Mose eyes the chips, but he knows better than to take them away from Esther. Nobody will be able to take the can without a fight. Esther's greatest weapon for getting just what she wants is her smile. If that doesn't work, she'll resort to her scream, which works every time. As the youngest girl in a family of nine children, her power knows no bounds. On Rebekah's instructions, Esther hands the can back to me so I can remove the foil cover, unveiling the chips.

Esther holds the can against her dress and grabs a fistful. Soon cheese dust spots her dress, taking its place alongside dried dirt and whatever she had for lunch. Esther wears a miniature version of her mother's simple whole-cloth dress, which covers her from her neck to her ankles. The dresses are usually dark

brown, blue, or green. No brightly colored dresses allowed. On
her head she wears a black organdy cap. No matter the day's
weather and regardless of the job to be done or play to be had,
the adults and children are always dressed the same. As early as
a few months old, children wear Amish dress, their cloak of
identity. Rebekah, twelve years older than Esther, wears an
identical outfit, only a good bit bigger than her younger sister's.
Mose looks like a little Amish man. He wears dark-blue pants
and a blue shirt. Suspenders hold up his zipperless pants, which
have side pockets with a single button. Mose's wide-brimmed
straw hat is battered, but his dad has promised him a new one.
A young Swartzentruber Amish girl down the road will make
him one for four dollars. The shirts pull over the head, and
there are two buttons down the front. None of these clothing
choices are arbitrary—all are according to the church's Ordnung, the rules, which govern everything from how wide a hat's
brim must be to the seam width on a woman's dress to what
tools can be used to how much money somebody can earn.
Mary makes every stitch of clothing her family wears: dresses,
aprons, caps, bonnets, pants, shirts, jackets, underwear.

The clothes are designed to mark their wearers as Amish.
The Amish wardrobe symbolizes the idea that no individual is
more important than any other, and that community trumps
individuality. Dress signifies that Gelassenheit, or gladly giving
oneself to tradition—a highly regarded value—surpasses any
modern fashion. Dress is one of the signs that communicates to
others that a person is Amish, separate from the rest of us, belonging to a community of believers, not a person so much as
an Amish person. Plain clothes quietly proclaim that a person is

already spoken for and therefore cannot belong to any other people or organization, and cannot swear oaths of allegiance to any other body, especially the state.

I do not doubt the intended symbolism of their dress, and I respect their beliefs immensely, but the more I get to know these people, the more difficult it is to see them as merely Amish. Perhaps it is my "Englishness" or my modern conceits or my American temerity that forces me to exalt the individual hidden beneath the clothes. Perhaps there is something about the human spirit that defies the notion of conformity and homogeneity. And yes, sometimes it takes me a couple of seconds to pick Samuel out of a crowd of identically dressed bearded men, but I do pick him out, just as I can identify his children running around at recess in front of their schoolhouse. No matter how similarly they are dressed, Rebekah is not Esther and Mose is not Andy. And Levi is not Samuel.

And while all Amish may appear to dress like all other Amish, there can be a myriad of differences among orders and church affiliations. Single girls of an Old Order group may wear white caps, but among the Swartzentrubers, only girls fifteen or older can wear them, and only around the farm, not to church. Only married women wear white caps at home and to church. As a Swartzentruber, whenever a girl or woman goes out on the road in a buggy, she must wear her black bonnet over her cap. Shaking his head at what the more modern Amish are getting away with, Samuel tells me that some Amish girls and women can forgo bonnets and wear caps while out on the road. Caps may be fine for around the house and on the farm, but out in public? Samuel finds this difficult to digest.

Rebekah and Daniel leave the snacking to Esther and Mose while they continue washing the pumpkins. Rebekah sticks the pumpkins in a tub filled with now dirty water and washes off dried dirt and caked mud. She then drops them into a tub of clean water, where Daniel runs a hand over them and then dries them off before placing them on the bed of another wagon.

As I watch Rebekah chatter with Daniel, as one splashes the other "accidentally on purpose," I can't help wondering if these two could have a future together. Daniel is tall for his age and quicker to talk to the English than a lot of Amish teenagers, suggesting an appealing confidence that might be attractive to a girl as capable as Rebekah.

"Have you come to help?" Daniel asks me.

Rebekah smiles, either at Daniel's aplomb or at the thought of my being any real help when it comes to farm labor.

"I'll help fill the bins," I say, not knowing if Daniel is serious, or what I am getting myself into.

Watching Rebekah and Daniel splash each other—harmlessly? flirtatiously?—it's easy to imagine they could end up together. They both belong to the Swartzentruber Amish. Marrying within one's settlement is acceptable, perhaps even preferable. It's certainly practical. Seventeen districts comprise the Lodi settlement, in which there are six church groups and ninety-three families affiliated with Samuel's group. With every family having between ten and fourteen kids on average, finding a suitable partner close to home shouldn't be all that difficult, which is not to say Amish won't travel to other settlements to find a mate. Samuel and Mary met at a wedding in Canada when he was living there and Mary was living in Ohio. Just the other day, Samuel's cousin, who's a member of a Swartzentruber settlement in Tennessee, was up here visiting Mary's youngest and only unmarried sister. "He's been sniffing around her for a couple of years now," Samuel says.

And despite the common public perception, Amish marriages are not arranged—young Amish folks marry for love.

But Rebekah and Daniel could not marry. Even though they went to the same school and are both Swartzentruber Amish and their families are good friends, Daniel's dad, John, split from Samuel's church ten years ago, which means he and Samuel belong to different affiliations. The only way Rebekah and Daniel could get married is if one joined the other's church, a cataclysmic event that probably would never happen. Changing church affiliations means excommunication and shunning to the Swartzentruber Amish.

Rebekah and Daniel are in what are often called the "learning" years anyway, between fourteen and seventeen years old (among the Swartzentruber Amish), when no dating is allowed. It's inappropriate for teens this age to even show an interest in members of the opposite sex. The learning stage is the time to do chores, help out in any way you can, and observe your parents and other elders.

Samuel chafes when he hears English talking about rumspringa, which has been sensationalized in the media with scenes of Amish kids having orgylike parties. Although some of the more liberal and modern Amish youth do participate in rumspringa at its most extreme, the more conservative groups do not, especially not the Swartzentruber Amish. For the Swartzentrubers in the Ashland County area, the years from seventeen until twenty-one are a time primarily spent with other kids their age, a span of years when finding a mate and preparing to join the church appear to be the ultimate goals.

✦ ✦

Because this is a Wednesday, Samuel and Mary plan to haul a load of produce to Homerville for the thrice-weekly auction. Pumpkins (orange, white, and even a few squat red ones), giant pear-shaped birdhouse gourds, butternut and acorn squash, and green and red peppers will be auctioned off tonight and the family has high hopes for the sale.

"We hope Samuel will have a good birthday and we'll get a good price tonight," Mary says.

Samuel turns thirty-eight today.

"I didn't even know it was my birthday until Mary told me this morning when we woke up."

Samuel says this as he finishes hitching up a team of plow horses who'll be pulling the wagon to tonight's auction. Daniel and Rebekah have swept out the wagon and it's ready to be reloaded, this time with large cardboard boxes. He walks the team up to the wagon, and he and Rebekah hitch up the horses. After Samuel finishes adjusting the reins and securing the hitch, he drives the wagon back to the barn. He returns with the empty boxes.

A cool southwesterly breeze blows through the afternoon accompanied by the sound of hammer on steel drifting out of Harvey Shetler's buggy shop just west of Samuel's house.

We load 202 pumpkins about the size of soccer balls into one box. Next it's the white pumpkins and squat reds.

Esther cries when she's made to leave the wagon.

Samuel dries off the wet reins on the tail of one of the plow horses. "Didn't know a horse's tail had more than one use, did you?" he asks me. "God made them to swat away flies, and I use them as rags." Samuel stands in the wagon as Rebekah and Daniel hand him white pumpkins, assembly-line style. Samuel counts them as he places them in the boxes.

Esther returns and screams for help getting onto the wagon, where she takes her place in the driver's seat, reins in hand. Mose joins her and they get lost in their toddler world, where all conversation is in Pennsylvania Dutch. Amish children do not learn English until they begin school at age six, so I have no idea what the two of them are saying. By the time Esther and Mose finish eighth grade, they'll be bilingual, just like their siblings and parents. I often think that Amish bilingualism could teach America and its immigrants something about the ability to become bilingual without sacrificing cultural identity. The Amish learn English because it's practical to learn English. Although they take their separateness seriously, they know the America surrounding them is filled with monolingual English-speaking people with little tolerance for those who can't speak the language. Another language is merely another tool. Generally, the Swartzentruber Amish I know have no compunction about speaking Pennsylvania Dutch, a dialect of German that is sometimes called Pennsylvania German or just "Amish," to each other, even when English are nearby. Although many people assume the Amish speak English only when conducting business or conversing with their non-Amish neighbors, the Amish I know are too pragmatic a people for that. Samuel and

Mary have told me that when they're alone with their family and discussing things they don't want the youngest children to hear—like which of the kids will be going for a trip into town and who will be staying home—they speak in English, secure in the knowledge that only the bilingual of their brood will understand.

When we reach 130 white pumpkins in a box, Samuel decides the box is good enough to take to auction. While we load, an English woman pulls up to buy vegetables from the Shetlers' produce stand. She asks about the peppers.

"They're four for a dollar," Rebekah tells her without missing a motion in our assembly line.

Samuel says something to Rebekah in Amish, but I do make out a couple of the words: masking tape. Rebekah disappears into the house and returns with the tape. Samuel binds a ripped box. They often speak in Pennsylvania Dutch, not to exclude me but merely because work orders like "hand me one of those" or "push this end of the box" are not imperative for me to understand if I'm not being addressed.

"Anything you have to sell that no on else has, that's better," Samuel says, fishing in his pockets for something. "If I had cows with three legs . . ." When he catches me watching him remove a small wrench and a pencil from his pockets he says, "My pants pockets are like a toolbox."

Soon I'm actually helping without embarrassing myself too much. While Esther and Mose converse in the driver's seat, Samuel and Daniel take their positions next to empty boxes on the wagon. Rebekah stands amidst a pile of acorn squash, and I situate myself in front of a mound of butternut squash. Soon we have a work rhythm.

"Is there anything special I have to look for?" I ask as I begin tossing Samuel the butternuts.

"Just don't pick any small, crappy ones," he tells me.

Soon I get the hang of it. I'm picking uniform sizes and Samuel hasn't rejected any yet.

"You're going to dream about butternut squash tonight," Samuel says.

A minute later the southwesterly wind kicks up, cooling beads of sweat on my forehead and blowing Samuel's straw hat to the ground.

When we reach one hundred squash, I ask Samuel if we're going for two hundred, hoping he'll say no. With my back beginning to ache, I attempt to hide the horror that is no doubt evident on my face when Samuel says the box will fit over three hundred. I smile as if this is exactly what I was hoping to hear.

He offers to switch places with me. "Your back's gonna hurt."

"I'll be okay," I lie.

Rebekah and Daniel laugh when he drops an acorn squash and it lands on Samuel's hat.

"We haven't dropped any yet," I say. "And we haven't smashed any hats either."

Everybody laughs. We're in a nice groove now. Acorn squash move from a pile on the ground to Rebekah's hands to Daniel's box, where they're placed and counted; and at my end, the butternut squash, a dirty yellow in the autumn light of a late afternoon, migrate from their pile to my hands to Samuel's. I find myself focusing not so much on the next squash I choose or on making a good throw to Samuel. What I do instead is focus on the arc of each squash as it flies up against the sky and lands in human hands; and as these things often do, the assembly-line tosses and catches achieve a rhythm and balance that borders on the beautiful. Perhaps it's because the weather is fair and the season is autumn, but suddenly I experience a paroxysm of joy—sheer, sharp unadulterated joy. I'm suspended between two worlds, an outsider in an outsider's world. I'm here with friends who consider themselves separate from the world but woven into the earth, while we all throw fruits of the earth to one another: seeds planted, sown, produce reaped and cleaned, soon to be sold, bought, and eaten. Toddlers play, teenagers laugh, a friend loses his hat, my back aches, and through it all the beauty and heartbreaking brevity of this life pierce me with their stunning certainty.

→ ←

Watching Samuel and Mary's children throwing squash, playing on the wagon, and counting pumpkins, my mind suddenly fills with thoughts of Sarah. It's hard not to wonder who she would be had she lived. The day I first learned of Sarah's illness sticks with me, and it's stuck with the glue of guilt. While I was standing in front of my house, I saw Samuel coming down our street in his buggy, his driver (a horse used only for the road) moving at a faster clip than usual.

"Sarah needs to see a doctor," he said.

"What's wrong?"

"I don't know. She's having terrible headaches."

Samuel caught me as I was about to pick up my oldest daughter from the airport. I told him that I couldn't take her today, but that if somebody else could I'd be willing to be on call from then on.

"I'll go see Bill," Samuel said, referring to one of my neighbors.

"If he can't do it, come right back and let me know," I said, hoping I would not have to figure out what to do with my daughter if somebody else couldn't take Samuel and Sarah.

I hurried to the airport, frustrated as I waited for my daughter to retrieve her baggage. I hurried home. Later that day I stopped at Samuel's to check on Sarah. He said that the doctor did not have much to report but had said she should be taken to a hospital for a thorough examination.

"I'm sure it's nothing," he said.

"Jenny and Katy both get these terrible migraines," I told him, hoping to ease his worries about Sarah. "Seems like the girls always get the worst of it."

Initially, I feared Samuel and Mary would rely on a chiropractor for Sarah's health-care needs. The Amish I know are suckers for the alleged healing power of chiropractors, who do far more than back work. An Amish person with a cold or the flu will seek the curative powers of a chiropractor. Whenever Samuel travels to see his relatives in Missouri or Iowa, he and his family stop in to see a chiropractor near Kansas City. A few years ago, Samuel complained of "stomach trouble." He waited to seek help until he knew he could see his Missouri chiropractor. By doing a few tests, the man discovered that Samuel was allergic to dairy, primarily milk and cheese. He told him to lay off the stuff for six weeks or so. Samuel did and hasn't had any trouble since. "I like him and trust him," Samuel said of Dr. Missouri. "He takes the time to explain things to you and he talks to you like a regular human being. He's not always rushing off somewhere." According to Samuel, his chiropractor is a threat to his "colleagues" in medicine. When a secretary of his became ill, she was rushed to the hospital, where she died. "Nobody told me this, but I wouldn't be surprised if the doctors at the hospital knew she worked for him and let her die to teach him a lesson," Samuel said. And then he quickly added: "But I guess God figured it was her time." The Swartzentruber Amish I know have a healthy distrust of modern doctors, and because they do not have health insurance, they use chiropractors or small health clinics for many of their needs. One old joke asks, "How do you get an Amish person to go to the moon?" The answer: "Tell him there's a chiropractor there."

They also draw from a large array of home remedies and folk cures. In the Amish newspaper, the *Budget,* a reader will find numerous ads for herbs and other organic supplements designed to help with everything from low energy to a tired mind. There's a pill for better circulation and one that will eliminate heart disease. When I told Samuel's father about my daughter's rare degenerative kidney disease, he said, "Lemons. Tell her to eat lemons. They'll fix her up." If lemons worked for one Amish person, word will spread and soon other families will be applying their healing properties.

And while Samuel believes in the necessity of inoculating his animals, not one of his children has had immunizations. According to Samuel, if something is supposed to happen to one of his children—and by "supposed to happen" he means if it's part of God's plan—then there's no point trying to immunize against it. Samuel went on to say that God doesn't really care what he does with his animals.

When I visited Samuel one Saturday afternoon a while

back, an Amish man stopped over to ask his advice. The man suspected his toddler son had appendicitis and sought the remedy Samuel and Mary had used on their young son Jacob. According to Samuel and Mary, Jacob has twice had appendicitis, and there's no point in telling them differently. Samuel told the man to first have the boy drink a special tea that would help empty him out. The next thing you do is apply a coffee enema. It worked for Jacob, Samuel told the man. So the man went home ready to give the panacea a try.

As much as the Swartzentruber Amish favor natural and folk remedies, Samuel and Mary seemed instinctively to know that what ailed Sarah was something bigger than anybody realized, although she was a child who seemed to live apart from the troubles of the world. Sarah appeared always to be smiling. A certain peace accompanied her. We all knew there was something special about Sarah. She was thin and lithe, a bit pale, a paleness that only enhanced her pretty face and elegant bearing. Like our daughter Katy, Sarah had poor hearing and had to adjust to wearing gigantic banana-shaped hearing aids. We'd often stop by the barn on a Saturday evening and find Sarah without her cap on, sitting on her uncrossed legs, her head tilted to one side, her long, just-washed hair drying in the setting sun. After the headaches started, Sarah would sit in the same spot she had used for hair drying, only now she sat with her head in her hands, trying to stifle the pain.

We soon learned that Sarah had an inoperable tumor on her brain stem. Although they had no health insurance, Samuel and Mary ended up getting Sarah admitted to Akron's Babies and Children's Hospital, where she got first-class care. Within days of diagnosing her, doctors inserted a shunt into Sarah's brain, designed to relieve some of the pressure and ease the pain. Despite their reliance on and belief in chiropractors, natural remedies, and folk treatments, Samuel and Mary gave themselves and their daughter over to the latest and best modern medicine had to offer.

It wasn't enough.

Every day Sarah was sick, somebody from my family, usually my wife, Dandi, and our daughters would stop over to visit her. The Amish I know converge on the homes of the sick in their communities, so we felt free to do so as well. Nobody suffers alone. One day my wife would bring over a tiny plastic split-rail fence; the next day she'd bring a toy cow to place in the fence, then a horse, chickens, and lambs, and pretty soon Sarah had built herself a replica of the homestead she would soon be leaving. Near the end, Sarah could eat only popsicles, and so every day my wife and daughters would bring her popsicles and a toy. Sarah's favorite toy appeared to be a pink-and-gray pinwheel. She'd often be seen holding the wooden handle in her frail fist, blowing lightly, watching the petals spin. Some of the toys would probably never be found in an Amish home, but the rules seemed to be suspended for a couple of months. Almost all of the toys disappeared days after Sarah's death.

On October 1, 2000, just four months after her first headache, Sarah died. She was nine years old. She would be fifteen today.

The next days a pall hung over everything: house and barn, farm and field.

On the night of the viewing, Samuel led us through a throng

of Amish mourners in his home, and like a heavy black curtain they parted to let us through. In a back bedroom, Sarah, dressed in her church clothes, lay on a board stretched between two wooden chairs. An elderly man I didn't recognize held a kerosene lamp above Sarah's face. Whether it was the glow of the light or the play of the shadows, or the old Amish man's wizened face, or the tears of strangers, or just that there were so many people huddled in a home to comfort two young parents, to commemorate a life and to commiserate over a life lost, I felt at that moment that there was something beautiful and holy at the center of Swartzentruber Amish life.

Over three hundred Amish attended Sarah's funeral. My wife and I were two of three English mourners. The funeral service was held in Samuel and Mary's home. As is the custom with home church, my wife and I were led in separate doors, men in the front, women in the back. This is not as sexist as it sounds. Swartzentruber Amish enter the church not as families but as separate members of a congregation. Upon entering church, a person has entered alone, so it's just that person and God. Once inside, we sat on wooden benches with members of our own sex. My wife and I didn't see one another for three hours.

It was at that time that I learned something about the Amish commitment to community. From the moment of Sarah's death, the community descended on the Shetler house and farm. Men and boys from the area performed all the chores, milking the cows, feeding the chickens, chopping firewood, even preparing the house for the winter. An English undertaker came to the house to prepare Sarah's body, but not without the help of the community. (Unlike Samuel's mother, who didn't want to be embalmed, Sarah was. "Because she died in late winter," Samuel says of his mother, "we were fine. If she'd died in the summer, I'm sure my dad would have had her embalmed.") It's a Swartzentruber custom for the family of the deceased to ask two or three male friends to help with and witness the undertaker's work. No one would ever dare decline this request. "I've never had to do that," Samuel says. "I hope I never have to. Nobody would ever even think about turning the family down. My brother had to do it, and he said it was brutal, mean. But we believe it's just a body and the soul is gone by then." Women and girls cleaned the house, cooked meals, and stocked the pantry with food. Another neighbor built an oak coffin. The coffin had a small section, something resembling a tiny door, that when opened revealed Sarah's ashen face. Samuel pulled me aside at the funeral and told me that the coffin was made out of the oak trees I had watched him clear off somebody's land a year before. He was just doing the guy a favor, and the guy said he could keep the wood. I recalled the day. Samuel had no specific use for the wood at that time, but he was sure he'd end up using it for something.

The community also played a role in paying the hospital bills, which were in the tens of thousands of dollars. Among the Amish I know, a community's commitment to its people acts as the surest kind of health insurance. Somebody from the church group, usually the oldest man, will go from farm to farm taking up a collection and everybody contributes what they can. And people contribute not only because they believe it to be their Christian and Amish duty, but also because, if it's God's will, they could easily find themselves in Samuel and Mary's sorrowful shoes and the community would be there for them. My wife and I contributed also, directly to Samuel and Mary, knowing that in some way we were at least peripheral members of the community. I've never admired the Swartzentruber Amish more than at the time of Sarah's death. For weeks and weeks Amish families visited the Shetler family, unannounced and welcome visits, always reminding them that to be a member of the Swartzentruber Amish is never to be alone.

Just a couple of weeks after Sarah died, the entire family boarded a buggy and went to visit her grave, which is on the farm of an Amish man five miles away. The location of Sarah's body, like those of other local Amish dead, is marked by a blank, white, shoe-box-size stone. Samuel explained that the kids were "feeling homesick for Sarah" and wanted to go see her. I'd never heard the word *homesick* used in this way, but it seemed perfect somehow. Now that Sarah was no longer alive, they longed to return to a time impossible to regain, embedded in a home irretrievably lost.

→ ←

As I watch Samuel take a final squash count, I wonder how often thoughts of Sarah arrive unbidden in his mind as he cuts hay, milks cows, plants corn. I wonder if the loops he makes around the pasture while he's plowing or mowing mirror the loops in his mind, those images and thoughts he least wants to see or hear, the ones that appear anyway, reminding him that they're always there, that they have power over him, that no matter what he does, no matter how many acres he farms, how many horses he owns, how many children he raises, how obedient he is, no matter how hard he loves his God, his family, and his people, he's nothing in the presence of the dark thoughts of a daughter's death.

But I know this is merely sentimental. I have no idea what grinds through Samuel's mind as he goes about his day. Our friendship has its limits. I don't have the audacity or the courage to ask him how often he thinks of Sarah. I do know that he's certain Sarah is with God, safe in a far better place than here.

The last time I saw Sarah before she went into the hospital for the final time, she was just inside the back barn door, leaning on a two-by-six board designed to let dogs, cats, and chickens out and keep horses and cows in. Barn swallows flew in and out above her head. The board reached across the opening at about chest height and ran the length of the door. Sarah stood right in the middle with her arms crossed on the barrier in a relaxed pose with her bare right foot resting atop her left. She stood there at the first hint of dusk, gazing out over the back acres of the farm as if she could see forever.

FOUR

"You be careful out among them English."

During those January days just after Jonas left, his joy was endless and his senses overloaded, even while, back home, the elders of his church pressured his parents to rein in, reclaim, or reject their son.

A couple days after he left, his friend Kathleen drove her Hyundai out in a snowstorm to bring him over to her place for a visit. With a fresh haircut and English clothes, including jeans, cowboy shirt, and cowboy boots, he went to his first movie, one he'd heard of and was eager to see. Unfortunately, when he, Kathleen, and a friend arrived at the cinema early that afternoon, they discovered that *The SpongeBob SquarePants Movie* wasn't showing until later that night. So instead of *SpongeBob,* Jonas's first ever movie was *Fish Tales.* His second was *SpongeBob.* He wanted to see it so badly they all stayed for the eight o'clock showing. Jonas went from seeing not a single movie in eighteen years to seeing two on the same day. He laughed so hard at the movies that day, tears covered his face. He's since become mad about *The Dukes of Hazzard* and *CSI.* "I watch that [*CSI*] about every night it's on." He also loves Westerns, particularly the old ones featuring Roy Rogers.

Bright colors, especially red and yellow, fascinated him.

Nearly every shirt he bought was red, yellow, or a combination of the two. "If anybody saw anybody with a red coat and red hat, they didn't have to ask who it was," Jonas said. His eyes also gravitated to glitter and anything else that sparkled. And stickers. The guy couldn't get enough of stickers. One day he was in a convenience store and had to use the restroom. In the restroom he saw a machine that looked like it had stickers for sale. The ones he wanted had a bucking bronco kicking up dust. Jonas wanted those stickers. A cowboy setting on a sticker was almost too good to be true. He dropped in his quarters, got his stickers, and walked back out. When he opened the package, he at first didn't know what he held in his hand. And then he realized what it was: condoms. "I thought, 'Oh, shit,' and I threw them to the floor." Jonas never thought to ask himself why the store would be selling cowboy stickers in a bathroom.

There were other things that rocked his world. He didn't know how to look up a number in the phone book, use a washing machine, cook a meal on a stove, use a microwave, log on to a computer, or navigate the Internet. Whenever I'd call Jonas on his cell phone he sounded like I'd called to inform him the world had ended. At first I wondered if I'd done or said something to offend him. It gradually occurred to me that because he had no experience talking on the phone, he had no familiarity with the fluctuations of tone that conveyed a welcome voice on the other end. He responded to every question he could with a monosyllabic answer.

But he could talk to Kathleen. Beginning with the time she picked him up and drove him home, they stayed up late talking night after night. Jonas proved a good listener. "I've always been able to trust him with the most sensitive things about myself, and it was important for me at that time to know that I could trust a guy," Kathleen said. For a while Jonas, Kathleen, and a friend of hers were the "Three Musketeers." They did everything together. They went to movies and the mall. Sometimes they just sat around talking, which is something Jonas didn't feel comfortable doing when Nora and her husband were around. One night they were talking about Amish dating, and Kathleen asked Jonas if he knew what a French kiss was. He said no, and when she told him what it was, "he made a face like a ten-year-old who was grossed out." After that night, Jonas occasionally brought up the idea of the French kiss to Kathleen. He grew increasingly curious. So one night Kathleen demonstrated on him, student and teacher. He was no longer grossed out. When Kathleen asked him if he was a virgin, he immediately said no, but then admitted that he didn't know what a virgin was. She explained, and he reluctantly admitted his true status.

It's hard for me not to see Jonas and Kathleen's relationship as symbiotic. He needed a docent in the modern world, one who would help him look and act the part of a nineteen-year-old English man. Kathleen had assumed the role of an older sister for him. She was conveniently close and just as conveniently out of reach. Kathleen needed a guy she could have as a friend, a guy she could talk to and confide in, somebody who would not always be trying to put the moves on her. Both relished their roles. A bit of Pygmalion was at work as well. Sitting on the back porch of the Gilberts' house with the two of them not long ago, I witnessed the dynamic at work. Because English is his second language, Jonas has a habit of pronouncing certain English words with Pennsylvania Dutch consonants. The *th* sound in the middle of the word *brother,* for instance, Jonas pronounces as a *d* sound. Another pattern Kathleen was trying to purge from Jonas's speech was the use of the word *already,* as in "I did that yesterday already." She also corrected his grammar, even though hers was far from perfect. When Kathleen asked me if I heard these aberrations in his speech, I said that I tried never to correct the grammar of anybody who speaks twice as many languages as I do. I believe Kathleen did have Jonas's best interests at heart. She cared for him like a brother. She understood how the shortcomings in his language and people skills could work against him when he applied for a job. I also believe she reveled in her role immensely, the way some older kids enjoy parenting younger ones when there are no adults around.

And yet just because Jonas had friends, wore jeans and T-shirts, carried a cell phone on his belt, and bore a symbolic tattoo on his arm didn't mean he was home free. He still had no proof that he was an American citizen, which meant no Social Security card, no driver's license, no legitimate job, no chance at taking the GED. In fact all he had was his short-form, un-official Canadian birth certificate. Because Jonas was born before November 14, 1986, and has at least one parent who was a U.S. citizen when he was born, he is technically a U.S. citizen. But he has not a shred of proof. He had to prove that his father, who was born in the States, lived here for at least ten years, and five of those years have to have been after he turned fourteen. For anybody else, proof of this was easy to garner. Not so for the

Swartzentruber Amish. Jonas could not prove his father had lived in the United States during the requisite years. Before Menno got married, he lived on his father's farm, and there was no proof of that except for his school records, which he had long lost or would not be willing to give up. The other course of action would be an affidavit, signed by Jonas's father, attesting to the fact that he had lived in the States during those years. Along with the fact that Menno could perceive signing the affidavit as akin to swearing an oath, which the Amish are forbidden to do, Menno was likely to refuse his son any help at all, except help returning home. The more he helped his son, the less likely it was that Jonas would return. The more trouble and obstacles refugee Amish face in the English world, the more likely they are to give up and go home.

Jonas at least wanted everything that was his. He had his short-form birth certificate, and he had gotten a copy of his father's birth certificate. Now he wanted his grade cards from school—they belonged to him after all—in hopes that they would offer some proof that he'd lived in the States most of his life. One day when his parents were away from home, Jonas sneaked back and talked to his younger sister, trying to persuade her to get him his grade card, showing he went to school in Ohio from first to eighth grades. His sister was wary, but finally she agreed to get the papers—after Jonas slipped her twenty dollars. I have to wonder what she did with this money. She couldn't give it to her parents, because they'd want to know where she got it. There's really nowhere to spend it unless she went to a store without her parents. Maybe she just wanted it because it was something she could call her own. Or maybe she wanted her pound of flesh from Jonas for leaving.

→ ←

A short time after Jonas left, he wanted to stop in and talk to his folks, just to let them know that he was fine and that nothing was their fault.

Later I learned that Samuel (in his twin roles of uncle and deacon) and his father had gone to see Jonas at his father's house the first night he showed up back home.

"We talked and talked. He just has no fear of God in him," Samuel said.

Jonas had his own version of what happened that night.

"I left the Amish and then I stopped in two weeks later," Jonas said. "I heard my family was really upset about it and I wanted to tell them why I left. The first time I came over they let me in. I waited until they were finished with dinner. And then Sam and my grandpa came in and my grandpa started yellin' about my haircut and my clothes."

Then Jonas's grandfather, Samuel's father, told Jonas's parents that they shouldn't let Jonas in the house.

"I wasn't scared of him," Jonas said of his grandfather. "That's the way he is. He's old, and if he thinks something it comes out of his mouth. Sometimes he would raise his voice, but I could see in his eyes that he wasn't mad. Even at church he would get all excited and raise his voice. Everybody laughed about it. I always enjoyed his company."

Jonas always liked to help Samuel more than anybody else.

Because Samuel's boys are too young to be of any real help when it comes to haying or mowing, he sometimes hires the son of a friend or neighbor to work with him. Samuel makes the arrangements by approaching the boy's father and asking if he can be hired out.

"I helped him a lot of times to get logs out of Cinnamon Lake (a local gated community). A lot of ministers were real serious. And Sam can be serious with other ministers. But when me and him were just together, we would joke around and stuff."

Because Jonas is the first person in at least two generations to leave the life, the entire family is "heartsick," and all ache for his return.

"I had long enough time to think about my family. I knew I was going to miss them, so I was prepared for that. After six months, I really missed them, and was sad about how hard it is on my parents that I left. There was about a day or two there when it really hit me hard. Then it went away and it happened again when I had been gone for a year. But if you have a steady job, it helps you not think about it."

I was struck again by Jonas's generous feelings toward his family and the life they lead. He'd been able to see something in his grandfather's eyes that maybe the old man didn't intend to convey. He talked about enjoying his time with Samuel. He seemed to understand the role the church has to play.

A few months later his attitude would change.

But on this first visit to his parents' home as an ex-Amish, he talked and played with his brothers and sisters as if nothing had happened. When they finished playing and Jonas was catching his breath, his mother told him that everything would be easier if he would just come back home.

Jonas said that if he came back, he'd have to leave again.

The visit lasted forty-five minutes.

According to Jonas's sister, the visits from ordained men and other baptized men continued. Nearly every night she would hear her parents arguing with the church representatives downstairs. These officials wanted the family to have nothing to do with Jonas, and they did not want them helping him in any way. Although Samuel didn't want to discuss his role in the church's pressuring of Jonas's parents, it must have been difficult. As a deacon and a minister, it would have been Samuel's duty to work with the church to make sure Jonas's parents knew how high the stakes were. To help Jonas in the slightest way would be disloyal and would be damning Jonas. The bottom line was this: Jonas would not be let back in the house unless and until he came home for good. And his father said he would not be able to see or be near his new baby sister or his other siblings.

→ ←

All Jonas knew how to do during all of this was work. At first he worked on a dairy farm, milking a couple of hundred cows a day. The pay was poor, and he was aching to work construction, not back on a farm. Later he worked at a county fair, but when fair season ended, so did the job. Then he heard about a guy with a construction crew who was willing to hire an ex-Amish kid without official papers. Around here almost everybody hires the Amish for wages far lower than they'd have to pay an English person with lesser skills. The Amish of Ashland County, Ohio, play a role similar to that of Hispanic illegal aliens in the desert Southwest. I buy firewood from an Amish guy who sells it far cheaper than I can get it anywhere else. A person building a new home will hire an Amish carpenter or bricklayer, knowing the price will be lower and the work first-rate. One guy went so far as to have Amish wire his house, which turned out to be a costly disaster, but one that's not without its ironic humor. I also believe some people hire the Amish because they know they can be trusted, and that they're prone to submissiveness and nonresistance in case something goes wrong.

So Jonas needed a job where he could be paid under the table, and one in which hiring a kid with an eighth-grade education wouldn't be a problem. The guy he started working for, Dan, was the friend of a friend of a friend, but Jonas wasn't about to be too picky. Because Jonas didn't have a Social Security number, finding a more legitimate job was impossible, and he needed the money. Plus he likes to work. Now Jonas can see what an easy mark he was for a guy like Dan. Dan knew to hire an honest ex-Amish kid with no Social Security number willing to work for less than most kids his age. The job looked good to Jonas, especially because the guy said he'd pick him up and drop him off every day, and Jonas had no driver's license, no car, no money.

When he first started working with Dan things seemed to be going all right. They worked a few days a week, and Jonas was paid in a timely manner. Soon things started to change. Dan often predicted a busy week, only to call Jonas saying he was having trouble with his truck or his back. Soon Jonas was working less and less, and the schedule was erratic at best. One day they had contracted to put all-new insulation in an elderly woman's attic because she feared moisture was getting in and

Dan was only too happy to confirm her fears—and charge her four thousand dollars to put in all-new insulation, even though the attic was free of mold or any kind of condensation. Worse yet, Dan installed only two strips of insulation. Fearful he'd get in trouble and not wanting to rip the woman off, Jonas told her that there was no mold, so the woman didn't pay. Dan was so upset he fired Jonas. When Dan rehired Jonas, the same things happened. Dan told another woman that they'd paint her porch for two hundred dollars, and then charged her five hundred instead. When the woman refused to pay the extra money, Dan used Jonas's hammer to damage her five-thousand-dollar whirlpool. Soon Dan owed Jonas hundreds of dollars in back pay. Despite the dishonesty, the erratic schedule, and the pay problem, Jonas worked with Dan for over four months. While Jonas worked with him, Dan tried to teach him how to howl at girls, and he flirted with every girl they saw, telling Jonas that he was trying to get their phone numbers for him.

"I wanted him to advertise in Ashland County," Jonas told me months after leaving Dan's employ. "But now I'm glad he didn't because then everybody would know that I worked for a loser."

But Dan wasn't merely a "loser." In his forties, five feet eight and nearly 240 pounds, sporting what Jonas describes as a "big, big, hanging belly," Dan soon proved to be much worse than a disorganized and dishonest boss. On the way to pick up Jonas for work one morning, Dan pumped fifteen dollars' worth of gas and then took off without paying. After work that same day, Dan stopped at his house and parked his Chevy three-quarter-ton pickup truck with Jonas riding shotgun. He hadn't even turned off the engine before a cop car pulled up behind him. The clerk at the gas station had written down Dan's license plate number and a description of the truck. All the clerk wanted was the money for the gas Dan stole, but the police wanted a bit more. It turns out that there was a warrant for Dan's arrest. Jonas didn't hear from him for quite some time, but when he called again, Jonas went back to work with him again.

Then, in late February while driving home from work, again with Jonas in the passenger seat, Dan was pulled over by the county sheriff. The cop told him he was speeding and had expired license plates, a cracked windshield, and no taillights. When the cop took his license and went back to his car, Dan turned to face Jonas.

"I have to talk to you so you won't be scared," he told Jonas. "I slept with a girl who was only fourteen, and she pressed charges. They say I'm a sex offender."

Dan told Jonas he'd served six months in jail and that the girl said she was eighteen.

When the cop came back to the car, he walked up to the passenger side and asked Jonas if he was all right. The cop asked him if he knew Dan was a sexual predator. Jonas said he'd just been told. When the cop asked him for identification, Jonas admitted he had just left the Amish and had no official paperwork. The officer believed Jonas because he could hear Amish in his speech. Jonas continued working with Dan for two more months. When Nora went on the Internet to see if Dan was a registered sex offender, she couldn't find his name, which Jonas took as a sign that everything was kosher. He needed the money and the guy had been paying him regularly, as least lately. Plus Dan picked him up every morning and dropped him off every night. A couple of days later, Nora learned that the guy used to go by the name Danny instead of Dan. And then she found him on the registered sex offenders list. Nora and Kathleen encouraged Jonas to quit, even saying they'd cover him until he could find another job, but he was adamant. "I didn't want them to take care of me. I don't like to be without a job."

Jonas trusted Dan, even after he learned of his past. "You don't know what you're talking about," he told Nora and Kathleen.

I can't help thinking of the Amish calling the outside world sinful, and how much this encounter with Dan played right into Amish expectations for Jonas now that he'd left the safety and sanity of the Swartzentruber Amish. Out for just a few months and Jonas was working for a guy who cheated the elderly, stole gas, violated young children. Sin everywhere you looked. Perhaps it was the devil doing his work to make Jonas come back, or maybe it was God showing Jonas the evil realities of the outside world.

I imagine hearing a whisper of the final words of *Witness* wafting in and out windows, under eaves, and along the furrows of Amish farms: "You be careful out among them English."

FIVE

The Midnight Table

I walk into a soggy field on the east side of the Shetler farm. Actually, walking is a euphemism for the awkward and futile hopping I do from one less-drenched spot to another. My goal is Samuel, Lena, and Bill. With the back pasture too wet to do anything with, Samuel is helping out in the smaller pasture, using one old horse, a hand-held plow, and a child. By the time I reach them, I'm in mud up over my ankles. My once-white tennis shoes resemble the wooden ones worn by Dutch children in storybooks. I give up. I surrender to the wet earth. Samuel holds down a hand plow as the old plow horse, Bill, plods through the dirt with nine-year-old Lena on his wide back. She waves and smiles, looking over my head for my wife or daughters. Realizing I'm alone, Lena returns her attention to Bill, grabbing his mane.

From the time she was a baby, Lena has exhibited a spunkiness and openness much like Rebekah's. She's a petite beauty who laughs easily and somehow smiles without using her lips. Her cheeks do all the work. She was the baby Mary was about to have when Samuel and I drove to Canada to attend his mother's funeral. Like all Samuel's other girls, Lena warmed to me gradually and only after being won over by my wife. Dandi can pin down the day her relationship with Lena changed. She had gone over to feed our horse, and Lena, three or four at the time, ran over to inspect the feeding. Dandi held oats in her hand that the horse lipped up. She then poured oats into Lena's hand and held it while the horse took the oats. Since then they've been friends. To this day, when she's home and free from chores, Lena shows up at Dandi's side, reaching out her hand, palm open, waiting to receive the oats.

My relationship with the girls demanded more than oats. The Swartzentruber Amish I know are as insular as any Amish order, and far more so than most. Getting inside the community is difficult. Because so few of them work off the farm, the opportunities for interaction with English are limited. If a family does have a relationship with the English, some kind of business transaction provides the reason. Ordinarily, socializing does not happen. But perhaps my status is no longer that of an ordinary English person. After all, my family is referred to by the Shetlers as "the Joes," just as families within the Amish community itself are known by the first name of the husband (the Shetlers are "the Samuels" or "the Sams"). Still, an English man truly getting to know and become friends with Amish women or girls appears to shock both cultures.

Not long ago I asked Mary if it would be okay for Rebekah to show me around their basement, because I was curious about how they stored their food without refrigeration. I know the girls trust me and my family. Whenever Samuel and Mary visit relatives in Tennessee and leave a few of the older kids behind, the kids don't want anybody to know they'll be at home without their parents. But they do want us to know. Still, I sometimes feel the tension of taboo when I'm alone with the girls. On the day I'm writing about, Rebekah led me to the basement, where the temperature had to be twenty degrees cooler than outside. She showed me the food stored in jars, which would provide the family's meals through the coming winter. There was canned bologna, sausage, hamburger, pears, peaches, plums, raspberries, strawberries, cherries, tomatoes, sweet corn, peas, pickled beets, cider, applesauce, canned pumpkins, dill pickles, sweet pickles, green beans, and bread. And it was all stored without refrigeration for months at a time. Mary cooks the hamburger, for instance, in its jar in boiling water for three hours before sealing the lid and storing the jar. Rebekah was explaining all of this to me as the two of us walked around the dark basement alone. She seems to talk more easily when she's with one person. In a group, even if that group is her family with us as company, Rebekah smiles often and answers questions but will generally not encourage conversation. We headed deeper into the daytime dark of the cellar. I was relieved when Mary came down looking for paint, and I couldn't help wondering if she really needed the paint at exactly that moment.

It's hard not to talk about the fruits of the earth right now, seeing that the ground is beginning to suck the shoes off my feet. I mutter a question about what Samuel hopes to accomplish today, and then I let him talk. I'm always at a loss for words about farming when I'm around Samuel or, for that matter, other Amish farmers (all farmers if I'm being totally honest). Although I have lived in rural Ohio for almost sixteen years, I grew up in the suburbs. Cities and suburbs feel comfortable. Farming is just one more mystery for me to try to solve. I ask questions of Samuel. I'm sure he's embarrassed for me much of the time: "What's that growing over there, cabbage?" "Lettuce." "Oh." "When do you plant the corn, early spring?" "June." "Oh." "What's spelt? . . . Oh." "What's the difference between hay and straw? . . . Oh." These questions are especially humiliating for me because the Amish are notoriously good farmers, being able to farm land others have given up on, and because of this, I often think Samuel must judge me ignorant indeed of the fruits of nature, of the stuff of the earth. "The Amish were among the first to understand the uses of rotation, manure, and legumes," writer and farmer Wendell Berry writes. "They keep a balance between livestock and crops. They benefit from exchanges of labor and other forms of neighborliness. In lieu of massive consumption of fossil fuels and electricity, they make the fullest possible use of energies available on the farm—of the wind, of draft animals, and, of course, of their own bodies." Berry goes so far as to call Amish farming "Christian agriculture, formed upon the understanding that it is sinful for people to misuse or destroy what they did not make." I've talked with Samuel about Berry, and he often asks me about him. I like to tell him that according to Berry the Amish prove that the foundation of our economy is false. "By living without such 'necessities' as automobiles, tractors, electrical power, and telephones, the Amish prove them unnecessary and so give the lie to our 'economy.'" I can imagine the Amish thriving even more in a post-petroleum age.

As I walk a few steps with Samuel, Lena, and Bill, Samuel

tells me that his family will be going over to Mary's brother's farm tomorrow to help him dig a footer for his new house, an example of the "neighborliness" of which Berry writes. It will be a family affair. Mary's other brothers who live here as well as her sisters and their husbands will all be there. The men will dig while the women prepare a lunch and socialize. It's this kind of social capital that is central to maintaining the community.

Mary's brother is one of seven boys in the family of fourteen. Mary is the second-oldest child and the oldest girl. She has six sisters. I ask Samuel if he and Mary would ever want to have fourteen children. A big family is a status symbol to the Amish, particularly the Swartzentrubers. While higher-church Amish have seven or eight children, the Swartzentrubers usually have anywhere from nine to fifteen, sixteen, or seventeen. Samuel comes from a family of twelve. Between Samuel's children and those of his sister, who lives a mile down the road, Mr. Shetler, Samuel's father, has twenty-three grandchildren nearby. When you count all the grandkids, he's grandfather to over eighty. Samuel says he'd have to sit down with Mary and start writing down names to get the exact number of grandchildren his father has. With the size of the average Swartzentruber family being so high, it's no surprise the Amish population in the United States has doubled in the last quarter century. Once Samuel told me that one old Amish guy we both know has only four children. "I don't know what's wrong over there," he said. "I guess the bedroom wasn't big enough."

Samuel's still pondering the thought of fourteen children. "They'd drive me crazy," he says.

I find this difficult to believe. There appears to be an ease between Samuel, Mary, and their children. They also trust their children to look out for themselves. Swartzentruber Amish—probably all Amish—stress obedience to parents. This obedience is a central credo of Amish life, and some call it the "first commandment," based on a selective reading of Ephesians 6: "Children, obey your parents in the Lord, for this is right. Honor thy father and mother; which is the first commandment with promise; that it may be well with thee and thou mayest live long on the earth." When Amish refer to this reading, they generally end it after "is the first commandment." The point gets made. Children are given a free ride during their first two years of life, but after that it's open season on spanking as punishment for disobedience. The Amish spank without compunction. The Amish children I know best are well-behaved and obedient, but they're still children. Jacob and Mose argue almost daily, just like any young brothers close in age. The two of them are in charge of feeding the hens and ducks, and each rarely thinks the other is doing his share. Just the other day, while Samuel put up drywall, Mose, Jacob, and Esther were going at it pretty good. Esther ended up crying. She disappeared, reappearing a few minutes later eating a Milky Way. No more tears. At least not for now. A summer day can stretch forever when you're a child.

"Yeah, I think they'd drive me crazy if we had that many," Samuel says again. After he says this, Samuel is quiet for a minute, except for commanding Bill to stop, as if preparing to say something important, something that can't be said while plowing. Or, I soon learn, something that is not for Lena's ears.

He walks a few feet away, ostensibly to show me how the corn is doing. "Mary's having another baby," he says.

When I ask if I can tell my wife, Samuel hesitates for a few seconds.

"Yeah, you can tell Dandi, just don't say anything in front of the kids." And by kids, Samuel means his kids.

"Is there a reason for that?" I ask, thinking that perhaps he's worried about Mary's health or that the doctor had said something about her having another baby now that she's in her late thirties.

"Yeah, there's a reason for it," he says. "I just don't know if I can say it in a way you'd understand."

He looks down for a moment as if the answer grew in the freshly plowed ground, trying to figure out, I assume, how he might word what he has to say. He's always careful this way.

I wait silently.

"We just don't want the kids to know anything about sex until they're older."

I ask if kids—all kids—don't talk or at least speculate about the nature and mysteries of sex among themselves, recalling some of the idiotic pubescent discussions in which my friends and I engaged. Samuel says that although he is sure most kids do talk, he surely did not.

"I thought things," he says, "but I never said them to anybody in case I was wrong. It was just my opinion. I had a few surprises when I got married." One surprise Samuel admits to was finding out that sex—more specifically reproduction—didn't work with humans just the way it did with animals. "I thought it was like cows and horses. You do it once and then they're pregnant. I guess humans are the lucky ones."

➤ ◄

Six months after our discussion in the field, on a cloudy morning in August with the humidity already pushing 90 percent, I drive to Kidron, Ohio, to pick up Samuel, Mary, and their new and tenth baby, David. Mary's doctor works out of a clinic in town that caters mostly to Amish and Mennonites of various stripes, as well as other patients without health insurance. The sky is beginning to darken as Ohio anticipates the rain promised by Hurricane Katrina.

The rain begins to fall now as I pass Amish farm after English house after Amish farm. A flock of grackles peels off the field on one side of the road and flies to the other as if they're all of one thing, a flying broad cloth of black. As I close in on the clinic, a bird, perhaps disoriented by the storm surging up from the south, smacks into my windshield, fluttering over the roof of the car and landing on the road, quivering. I could take it as a bad omen—of what, I don't know. I do know that it's difficult to have too much respect for a bird in flight that gets hit by a car. Maybe I've spent too much time with my Amish friends, who are not so quick to anthropomorphize beasts.

The rain's coming down hard now and I check for my umbrella so I can shield Mary and the baby. No sense in a brand-new tiny human being getting baptized with the offspring of a dangerous hurricane his first time out in the world. I have visions of Mary, Samuel, and the baby standing huddled in the rain as they wait for a car ride they do not like having to take, their other children gazing out the windows at home waiting for the wonder of yet another sibling. If they had to ride home with the baby in a buggy, the ride would take a full six hours rather than the forty-five minutes it will take us by car.

As I drive I smile, remembering Samuel telling me about the "surprises" he had when he got married. Although the majority of Swartzentruber Amish grow up on farms, where they're exposed to the often brutal yet natural world of animal coupling, they receive no sex education, no anatomy and physiology instruction, which explains Samuel's surprise. Samuel told me he was also surprised by the fact that women had menstrual cycles. "I had no idea," he said. "I only had two sisters, so I didn't get the chance to see a bunch of sick girls all the time." Samuel looked over at Jacob and Andy, who were playing near the pasture gate. "We just don't want them to know anything about sex until they're married. Nothing wrong with not knowing everything. I like surprises."

And yet the dating rituals of the Swartzentruber Amish could be considered scandalous. When a Swartzentruber Amish youth turns seventeen, he or she is allowed to hang out with other "young folks." The young folks, generally ranging in age from seventeen to twenty-one, get together on Sunday evenings after the day's worship. After all the married couples and their families have left, the young people stay at the home that held the church services. At around seven o'clock, the boys will sit on one side of a long wooden table and the girls will sit on the other. As they face each other, they sing hymns in Old German from their hymnbooks. The singing usually lasts for two hours, and then the dating begins.

A boy will approach a girl and ask her to "have a date." When she agrees, she and the boy will ride in his buggy to the girl's home. When they arrive they go straight to the girl's bedroom, where they lie, fully clothed, all night long. That's quite a first date. Throughout the night they talk and get to know each other. Falling asleep is a good way to have a bad date. I asked Samuel and Mary if this lying in bed all night could be tempting fate; they both said that the youth are trusted to remain chaste, not even touching. It's generally believed that only the Swartzentruber Amish and a few Old Order groups still date this way, which is considered very old school even among the Amish, a tradition whose day has come and gone. But as with many others, the Swartzentrubers of Ashland County hold tight to this tradition, which is a form of the old European practice called bundling.

And yet even among the Swartzentrubers dating practices can vary. A church group from the settlement near Bowling Green, Kentucky, practices another form of bundling. Rather than lie in bed fully clothed all night, these Swartzentrubers will remain upright. Sort of. The guy will sit in a rocking chair made of hickory and oak, and the girl will sit on his lap, all night long. Barbara, a Swartzentruber Amish girl from Kentucky who left the Amish five months ago, says that "having a date" was one of the main reasons she left. In her district girls sat in the boy's lap in a hardwood rocking chair all night. "I would go on a date if we went out, went somewhere. I'd even rather talk in bed than on a rocking chair." Some Old Order Amish go back to the girl's home, where they sit in chairs facing each other and talking for a few hours. But the Swartzentruber Amish of Samuel and Mary's church group have stayed with the old ways.

Hanging out with the young folks is as close as the Swartzentruber Amish get to rumspringa. One young ex–Old

Order Amish woman named Lilly from Holmes County told me that the day her brother turned sixteen he got his driver's license and a cell phone. He bought a car not long after that. Next began the drinking and partying. According to Lilly her parents are not happy about the brother's English actions, but they're letting him run around, hoping that he'll get this behavior out of his system in a few years and then join the church of his own free will.

"I hope that rumspringa never comes here," Mary has said more than once.

→ ←

Samuel recalls his first date. He was just seventeen and the woman was twenty-one. "She was okay, but because she was so much older I didn't think it would work out. She married my cousin, so she must not have thought I was too bad. She was just a little thing. Whenever I see her, I can't help wondering how things would be if we'd married."

For Mary, the year she turned seventeen was difficult. After living on a farm in Fredericksburg, Ohio, her family moved to Ashland County. At first it was tough for her because she was part of a group of young folks, and she had just turned dating age. "It had its good points and bad points to make a move like that. As long as I could remember I was living on that farm. I was just starting to go with the young folks, but I figured there were lots of boys up here."

Samuel and Mary began dating just after they met at a wedding in Canada. Mary was asked by a male friend of hers to be a "witness" at his wedding. Witnesses are akin to bridesmaids and groomsmen, but there are only eight total, four for the bride and four for the groom. Usually the bride and groom pick the witnesses together. The wedding, like most Amish weddings, was on a Thursday. Samuel likes to say he knew right away that there was something special about Mary. Mary liked Samuel but didn't understand at that time just how much Samuel liked her. Although Mary was scheduled to go back home the next day, a snowstorm blew in and nobody could go anywhere. "I'm pretty sure Samuel asked me for a date that next Sunday night. And the snowstorm . . . it was like blame it on that. I was really surprised he wanted more," Mary says of Samuel.

Mary was telling me this one June morning as she sat on the floor of her front porch washing cabbage in a stainless steel bowl before tearing it up and placing it in a second bowl. Coleslaw is a staple at the Shetler table. I sat a few feet away, leaning on a wooden post. We were having this discussion on a bright summer day, late in the morning. Rebekah, Barbara, and Clara were inside the kitchen preparing lunch, and Mose and Esther were in and out, asking their mother questions. Mary interacted with her children in an uninterrupted rhythm. In Pennsylvania Dutch she told Esther to pick up the Snickers wrapper she had dropped, while asking the girls in the kitchen about all the banging we'd been hearing on and off for the last few minutes. She chatted with English people who stopped at the produce stand—in English. Samuel was not home. "Samuel said he'd be home by lunch," Mary said. "But you know men." And because Samuel was not home, Mary took a risk in talking to me. Although she knows and trusts me, the Swartzentruber Amish who ride by in their buggies gave her curious looks. I wondered if tongues would wag. Here was the minister's wife, sitting, talking, and laughing on her front porch with an English man while her husband was away from home. I had to wonder how much worse it would be if they knew what we were talking about. Rarely do Swartzentruber Amish women socialize with non-Amish men without being in their husband's company. Conducting a business transaction at the produce stand is one thing, but this . . .

As we talked that June day, several English people dropped by to purchase strawberries for a $1.25 a pint. For two weeks every June, every Amish farmer sells strawberries, and they sell like mad. Earlier, I had heard Mary hollering to her neighbor across the street. The neighbor, John, hollered back. Mary told me that she had run out of strawberries but that one of John's fourteen children would be bringing some over. Although John lives right across the road and is good friends with Samuel and Mary, he does not belong to their church because of a disagreement that occurred over ten years ago now. After Mary and I had been talking for another half hour, John brought over the strawberries himself. Although I know John, I still had the feeling that he was checking me out, or checking up on Mary. He was polite. We joked. He told me my hair looked whiter to him, which meant I must be thinking too much. "One old Amish has a long, really long white beard, even though his hair is dark," John said. "We tell him his beard's white because he talks too much." John stayed for a few more minutes before walking back across the road to his farm. I looked for any sign that Mary was suddenly uncomfortable. I saw none and she went right on talking.

"We'd have a lot more berries if the birds would leave us

alone. At first they were always here. Lately they're not around so much. I don't know if the birds are fed up with them or what."

→ ←

She and Samuel started dating when she was eighteen and he nineteen. At the time, Mary lived in Ohio and Samuel in Canada. For almost three years, until he was twenty-two and Mary was twenty-one, they dated when they were together and wrote letters when they weren't. "He came down awhile before we got married," Mary says of Samuel. "And I was up one time. I have an uncle living up there and I worked for him a bit." When separated by a border, Samuel wrote Mary a letter every week for almost three years. And then, in February of 1990, they married.

Like all Amish weddings, Swartzentruber weddings are an all-day affair, beginning at eight in the morning, an hour earlier than Sunday church or communion. The service is held in the home of a neighbor. At eight the singing begins. When the singing is under way, the bishop and ministers retreat to another room, where they plan the day, deciding who will do what job. The couple to be married joins them to, in Samuel's words—words that burst through his laugh—receive "the final secrets of married life."

The bishop then relates to the couple the story of Tobiah and Sarah, a version of which was sung by the congregation in Old German earlier that morning. It is clearly an understatement to say Sarah had had bad luck in her previous attempts at marriage. She has married and buried seven husbands. All of her husbands died on the night of their marriage, just before the couple were to consummate their nuptials. The angel Raphael wanted to bring Tobiah and Sarah together, so he told Tobiah to use a fish heart and liver to drive off the demon Asmodeus, the spirit responsible for killing Sarah's seven previous husbands. Sarah's father, Raguel, is delighted about the marriage and has high hopes for its success, but just in case, he has his servants dig a grave in which they can lay Tobiah if he dies, before the family becomes a laughingstock in the community. Tobiah does as Raphael tells him. He weds and beds Sarah and lives to tell about it. Raguel tells his servants to refill the hole in the ground. Sarah and Tobiah live long, happy, and prosperous lives. Tobiah reaches the ripe old age of 117.

I tell Samuel that this story sounds like an ominous one for a would-be groom to hear on his wedding day. He insists it's a rough story in places, but in the end everything works out and that's the point, and that the couple also hear about the marriages of Jacob and Abraham. Plus, in the scene where Sarah's father is telling Tobiah about her previous husbands, he also says, "She is yours according to the book of Moses. Your marriage to her has been decided in heaven!" Just as God chooses which men are ordained, he has a hand in choosing a bride for a groom and vice versa, which makes divorce unheard of among the Swartzentruber Amish.

When the bishop, minister, and couple rejoin the church group, the minister usually preaches, starting with Adam and Eve and moving on to the Great Flood. A bishop then takes over, going from the Great Flood to the end of the Old Testament, just hitting the highlights. When I ask Samuel if the New

Testament is next, he replies, "No. Just the Old Testament. The bishop hits the New Testament hard at communion."

At around noon the couple is married. A huge meal, which is served at the bride's house, follows the service. When the meal is over, usually just over an hour later, the church resumes singing, which goes on for all of the afternoon and into early evening. Another meal is served at seven, and then there is more singing until ten. Most of the guests, including all the married couples, go home when the singing ends at ten. Only the immediate family and all the single young men and women stay after that. When you're in the immediate family "you get to tease the boys and girls who are part of the midnight table. We tell jokes, clean ones, and laugh a lot," Samuel says. Although weddings usually take place on Thursdays, the couple will remain "pure" until Sunday, when they will consummate their marriage, a custom that is connected in some way to the story of Tobiah and Sarah. The young folks stay around for the "midnight table," which is held on wedding nights only, and is a figurative table. While boys sit on one side of the room and girls on the other, three boys called "hostlers," appointed by the bride and groom, act as aggressive middlemen. A boy will tell a hostler which girl he wants, and the hostler will approach the girl and tell her the boy's wishes. The hostlers will first hook up couples who are going steady, and then they will arrange the others into pairs. Theoretically, a girl could refuse a boy. I say theoretically because when I asked Samuel and Mary what would happen if a girl said no, neither had an answer, but they were sure it was permissible. After the midnight table, the couples "have a date," in bed, fully clothed, all night long.

→ ←

"You know what we did for our anniversary?" Samuel asked me a few days after he and Mary celebrated their sixteenth wedding anniversary. "Mary worked over at her mom's house and I shoveled manure."

There are a couple of family weddings coming up, one in Iowa and one right here. His oldest brother's daughter is getting married at age twenty-five.

"She's a little overripe," Samuel said, chuckling. "But she found somebody who's twenty-five too."

Because Samuel and Mary got back not too long ago from visiting family in Tennessee, they're not going to make the Iowa wedding. Samuel says they'll see everybody when they all come in for his niece's wedding a week from this Thursday.

Samuel's younger sister, her husband, and their daughter will be attending the Iowa wedding.

"She's eighteen," Samuel says of his niece. "She doesn't have a boyfriend as far as I know, so she might as well have a 'For Sale' sign on her when she goes to that wedding."

Whenever people ask me about the Amish and their marriages and families, and after they tell me they've heard all about rumspringa and shunning, they mention inbreeding. There appears to be no doubt that some Amish over the years have been involved in what are often called "close marriages," which is basically anything closer than and including second cousins. John A. Hostetler has written about the "inbreeding coefficient" in Lancaster County, Pennsylvania, and the "genetic drift" in Holmes County, Ohio. The Amish I know best are careful to avoid these close marriages, but the appearance of intermarriage is hard to deny. For example, Samuel's first cousin, who's up from Tennessee, is dating Mary's sister. One of the cousin's brothers is married to one of Mary's sisters. Mary's uncle, who was widowed early, married a young widow. Their two families came together, creating a family with twenty-one children. The oldest of the stepchildren were seventeen and eighteen. Knowing each other well, the stepbrother and stepsister married. If one brother has had success marrying a girl with a lot of sisters, the other brothers might be interested in getting to know the other sisters. Everybody seems tied to everybody else in one way or another. Mary's step-uncle lives down the road from her father and brother. The guy I buy my firewood from is Mary's uncle. Samuel's sister is just up the road from Samuel and Mary. Samuel's brother-in-law's brother is Samuel's bishop. I can drive past eighty farms and encounter only eight surnames: Gingerich, Yoder, Miller, Hostetler, Swartzentruber, Shetler, Stutzman, and Weaver. And on it goes. Even beyond the question of intermarriage and inbreeding, there is the fact that every Amish person seems to know every other Amish person.

→ ←

Although Samuel gave me adequate directions to the clinic, I fear I have taken a wrong turn. My sense of direction is woefully bad, humiliating, in fact. Getting lost with my wife in the car gives me a much better chance at arriving where I've actually set out to arrive. My inadequate sense of direction is one more thing Samuel likes to tease me about. Although I've lived in northern Ashland County longer than he has, he knows shortcuts into town I've never dreamed of. He knows which county road runs into which township road. I credit much of this to his not having the luxury of getting lost. Every extra mile out of the way is at least ten minutes of time, plus the wear on horse and passengers. When I do finally locate the clinic, Mary is still in with the doctor, but Samuel comes out to the waiting room to tell me it will just be a few minutes.

After he tells me that Mary and the baby are doing fine and looking forward to going home, he remarks that he used the microwave in the little kitchen area, the way I might tell somebody that I just flew to Europe on the Concorde. Although the Amish are forbidden to have electricity in their homes, they're also a practical people. The clinic has no cafeteria, and Samuel and Mary have been there for three days. He's had no buggy for three days. The food he packed is gone and the food in the vending machine is sparse. He used the microwave to cook some kind of burrito.

Mary comes out of the room with the doctor and pulls back the black baby blanket, and I get a peek at David's black hair and dark sleepy eyes. David is Mary and Samuel's tenth child, although only nine are living. And David is boy number four.

Samuel helps Mary into the backseat of my car; he takes the passenger seat and we head out. Soon Mary's asleep and Samuel begins talking with the chattering energy of a tired new father. He gives a running commentary on the farms we pass: who has a good field of beans, which farmer needs to get out and purge his garden of weeds. Perhaps because he has been away from his own farm for three days, he begins talking about a farmer's fear of too much rain.

"I'd like to live somewhere where they're not cutting up farmland," Samuel says. "I'd like it to be farmland all the way to a little town. That's how it is out west." And later: "If you're going to be a farmer, I've been thinking about this more and more, why move up north? You need more feed for cattle. You need more firewood."

It sounds to me as though Samuel's caught up in the dream euphoria of a fresh father, telling himself that it's still possible to move, that he's still young, that he's living a good Swartzentruber Amish life, that he's not finished living yet, that there's still much he can do. He can have more children, build a bigger house, take better care of his family, maybe even outrun the pain of Sarah's death.

As a state trooper passes us I worry that the baby's not in a car seat. I look in the rearview mirror to check on the trooper's progress. He's soon out of sight. And then I spot the baby asleep in his sleeping mother's arms. I worry about Mary because I know she almost always gets carsick. (Samuel boasts that he's never gotten carsick in his life, and I tell him I've never been buggy sick.) I try not to make any sudden swerves or stops. But the drive appears to be going okay. In the next instant Mary is awake, pulling back the corner of the blanket and peeking at David. All is well. Everybody's safe. When we arrive home, the kids all scurry out of the house and swarm their new brother. And a few minutes later he's sleeping in a cradle covered by a light cloth that acts as netting to keep the flies off. In the summer, flies are as ubiquitous on the farm as chores and chickens. A ray of sun shines on him, highlighting the black scab of his belly button.

→ ←

I leave Samuel, Lena, and Bill in the wet field, in a world where David does not yet exist, and slog my way to my car. I hear Samuel give Bill the command to walk, and the one to stop. The reasonable part of my brain tells me to take my shoes off and keep the car and my home free from mud. This thoroughly modern part of my brain tells me I should wear barn boots when I'm here, so I can make treks onto the farm, talk to the kids, share a laugh with Samuel, leave with a warm loaf of Mary's homemade bread, and get out clean.

But some other part of my brain—the part that loves the idea of daylong weddings and midnight tables—says, To hell with the mud on your shoes. Carry a part of the Shetler farm home with you. Give yourself to a world where production trumps consumption, where the past is as pertinent as the present, where holding on is more important than letting go, where obedience, humility, and peace are treasured. Give yourself to a world that prizes old ways and nonrevisionist history, where time is upended and technology suspect, where sacrifice defeats desire. Give yourself over to the un-American and subversive sentiment that what the individual wants is far less important than what the community needs. Let these tenets of Amish life stick to you like mud. Stop pretending that everything has to be clean and right and easy and careful and calculated and controlled. Give yourself to an Amish moment, a moment of mud and horses and hay and earth.

And so I do.

SIX

Underground Railroad

When he had been out for about a year, Jonas began changing. He became more fatalistic about ever getting his citizenship papers. He worried about deportation, because of all the talk he'd been hearing about an alleged crackdown on illegal immigration. It also seemed to Jonas like he had been out long enough for his parents to realize he'd never be coming back, so they should help him in any way they could. Jonas's parents no doubt knew how many young Amish have gone astray and then come home because they can't find a job and so don't have money for a place to stay. Jonas had been lucky. He has had a roof over his head the entire time, thanks to the Gilbert family.

Except for the times he was alone with Kathleen for late-night talks, when Jonas first moved in it was as if he didn't feel he could really trust the Gilberts. He was tentative about what he did and said. He rarely spoke and only answered questions with single sentences, if that. He wouldn't voice his opinion about anything. For several months after moving in during the early fall of 2005, Jonas stayed in an extra room. The talk was that when Jonas got proof of citizenship and a job, he'd move out. He had hoped to have his driver's license, a job, a car, and a little money in a month or two, but things hadn't worked out the way he'd planned.

All this is not to say that there had not been good times. His first Christmas away from the Amish and with the Gilberts, Jonas was as happy as the family had ever seen him. He wanted everything to be just perfect. He helped decorate the tree and bought everybody gifts. He spent hours setting up a Christmas village, making sure every house was lit from within. The Swartzentruber Amish celebrate their Christmas on January 6, the Epiphany. December 25 is a day the kids might get a pencil as a gift from their teacher and the day's work is light, chores only. No tree, no lights, no feast. So Jonas wanted to do his first Christmas right.

Just a few months later, however, things started getting rough. After quitting his job with his felonious boss, Jonas was owed close to $1,500 and knew he'd never see it, and he was still living with the Gilberts, taking care of the horses and the barn as a way to contribute and to keep busy. After weeks of being between jobs, Jonas told Kathleen and Nora that if he couldn't find a job soon he'd have to move out. "I said it just to see what they would say. They said that as long as they were working, they would take care of me. I don't know what I'd do without them. Guys my age who do stay out had some family take them in like it was their own kid."

Jonas spent his days cleaning the stalls, feeding and watering the horses. He wasn't working too much with his horse, Ashley, because he wouldn't be showing her until the fall. He liked to watch horse-training shows on the Gilberts' satellite TV and loved the idea of horse whispering, which is clearly not the way Amish train their horses.

He hadn't talked to anybody in his family for months.

"I just wanted to go see them and visit," Jonas said of the family he had left. "I'd like to take them all out to dinner, but I know that will never happen. I think with time, maybe they will let me back in. I want them to do what they think is right because that's what I'm going to do. I want them to have peace too."

Jonas had begun to change in other ways as well. He'd become more confident and self-aware, and with this came arrogance, a side of him Nora and Kathleen had not seen before. Where before he couldn't express his feelings, he was now able to say, "I'm hot, I'm tired, I'm hungry, and I'm really stressed out." Although Jonas still did what he was asked to do around the house, he now questioned Kathleen and Nora, telling them, "There's no need to do it," but then he'd do it anyway. Nora believes she has picked up on a darker side of Jonas. Anything a man tells him, he believes, just like he believed Dan for all those months, even while Kathleen and Nora were telling him the guy was no good. Nora viewed Jonas's behavior to women as expressing a "What do *you* know?" attitude. When she, Jonas, and Kathleen attended horse shows where Jonas showed Ashley, he might lose points from the judges because he failed to line up right. When Nora and Kathleen told him what to do next time, he wouldn't listen. He was a guy and he'd do it his way. I have to wonder how much of this is being nineteen years old and how much of it derives from being bred in a severely patriarchal society.

Other things were changing too. He was no longer as interested in taking care of the horses and the stalls. He slept late, sometimes until close to noon. He and Kathleen argued more;

he was growing tired of her questions and opinions. According to Nora, Jonas also thought he could dress like a cowboy and women would come running. Jonas posted his picture on a website called "Hot or Not," where women would write in and rate his looks. Jonas was not happy with the results. Whenever he fell for a woman he met, he'd fall hard and instantly. When he met Kathleen's cousin, he fell for her so hard that he "followed her around like a puppy." She wasn't interested. What Jonas would not do was date an ex-Amish woman. Not ever. Dating an ex-Amish woman would be to admit he'd never really be English, that the most he'd ever be was ex-Amish. No, the woman would have to be English.

After being out for a year, he was still a long way from where he wanted to be. He was still without a job or a girlfriend. He had managed to acquire his long-form official birth certificate from Canada, but he still had no proof of his father's residency. He was really no closer to a passport, which would help him get a Social Security card. His driver's license seemed farther away than ever. He needed more help.

→ ←

There is a netherworld between the Amish and the English, an uncertain oasis, an unofficial way station made up of nascent ex-Amish and those who have been out longer, those who have made it in the English world. An ex-Amish kid with a place to stay will offer his floor and his food to a kid who's trying to get out. It's an ex-Amish version of the Underground Railroad.

The most well-known stop on this railroad is the organization called Mission to Amish People (MAP), which was founded by Joe Keim in 2000. Joe and his wife, Esther, left an Old Order Amish sect almost twenty years ago. Since leaving the Amish, the Keims have helped over a thousand people cross over to English life. At least one hundred have actually stayed in the Keims' home. They have housed ex-Amish from as far away as Wisconsin, Iowa, and Texas, and MAP has placed Bible study packets in some two thousand homes in Ohio alone and thousands of others in every state where you'll find Amish. Six years ago they made their calling official and MAP was born. MAP is an Ashland-based organization designed to help ex-Amish find housing and clothing and get birth certificates, Social Security cards, and driver's licenses. MAP also helps ex-Amish earn their high school equivalency. A room at the church where Joe is a minister serves as an ex-Amish Goodwill, where people donate clothes for Joe to give Amish kids for free. Most important, Joe and Esther hope they can bring ex-Amish to Christ, while leaving the strictures of religion and the confines of Amish life behind. Joe still talks with a heavy Amish accent even though he's been out for two decades. His sixteen-year-old son, Jonathan, a computer expert of the highest order, also speaks with the accent, even though he's never been Amish.

Joe, who has a reputation as an honest, caring, and serious person, says his mission is simple: "I've never been out to destroy the Amish. I just want to help people who want to leave, who don't want to live that way. We even encourage parents to come and if the person wants to go back, we support them."

Like all ex-Amish of the area, Jonas had heard of Joe Keim. Along with being the founder of MAP and a minister of his own church, Joe is savvy about both worlds. Because Joe and

Esther left after they were baptized and married, they have been excommunicated and shunned. When Joe's grandmother died not long ago, he received a letter saying he would not be welcome at her funeral. He stayed away. When Jonas explained the problem of not being able to get a Social Security number or a passport, Joe suggested he dress Amish, go into a local Bureau of Motor Vehicles office and ask for a state identification card. According to Joe, the bureaucrats hardly ever question the Amish, and this ploy had worked often over the years. It had worked so well, in fact, that one BMV site has barred Joe from entering. He'd been in there too many times with too many Amish kids. Jonas seemed eager to let Joe help him obtain his Social Security card, but as soon as Joe asked if it would be okay to visit him for Bible study, Jonas stopped returning Joe's calls. Jonas said he was afraid to take any shortcuts, in case a decision made now would come back to haunt him later. He also said, "I don't want to go to church. I want nothing to do with church."

Joe admits that it hasn't always been easy, especially with the Swartzentruber Amish. One ex-Amish girl the Keims took in wrote a list of all the things she wanted to accomplish now that she was no longer Amish. The items on her to-do list included "have sex with a dozen different guys," "kiss a nonwhite guy and then have sex with him," "shoplift," "make out with a married guy," "make out with a divorced guy," "get pregnant," "drink and drive," "do drugs," "beat up a girl," "lose twenty-five pounds," and "try to commit suicide."

"These people are forced to live one way, and when they leave they just explode," Keim said. "They don't want any authority at all. The more legalistic they are—like the Swartzentrubers—the further out they go. Sometimes it's hard," Joe said. "I've been up bawling my eyes out until five in the morning because I can't reach some of these kids."

All Amish who seek refuge with Joe are required to sign a household policy contract. At the very top of the contract, Joe lays out his mission: "Our family is glad we can share our home with you. It is our desire to make your stay with us as comfortable and enjoyable as possible. It is also our desire to help you get on your feet by helping you get a job, a driver's license, car, and finally your own apartment (we may not always be able to help you personally but we will try and find the help that you need)." The contract then lays out what's expected of the boarder, including rent. The Keims charge twenty-five dollars a week if the person has a job, nothing if he or she does not. It's fifty dollars a week for tenants who eat with the family, if they have a job. The downstairs apartment is usually home to three newly ex-Amish. For a while it was guy after guy, then Joe noticed a sea change in the ex-Amish he was putting up. "For the first fifteen years we had no girls living with us. I didn't really know too many girls who left. For the last few years, it seems like all we've had are girls staying here." Kids of either gender are expected to attend prayer meetings once a week and church every Sunday. "On Sunday morning everyone goes to church," the household policy reads. No exceptions. Other rules are standard: keep the place clean, easy on the electricity, and then the other biggies—no opposite-sex sleepovers, and "drugs and alcohol are never allowed in our home or on our property. Sex outside of marriage is absolutely not allowed in our home or on our property."

I've asked Joe many times if he believes there are Amish people who want to be Amish right down to their marrow, people who love the life and see it as full and free, as I believe the Shetlers do. Joe doesn't believe there are any true believers, not really. "Nobody likes to have the preachers and family and neighbors in their lives all the time. If they could come out and really experience freedom, nobody would want to live under that bondage. That's not how God made us."

When I asked Samuel about Joe Keim, he seemed not to know who I was talking about, although I'd assumed Keim must be notorious among Amish parents and the ordained. "I know there was a Keim who moved to New York who had some sons who'd left the Amish," Samuel said.

We left it at that.

→ ←

Having rejected Joe's help, Jonas continued picking up odd jobs and worrying about how he'd ever get his papers. He had no money to hire a lawyer. His parents wouldn't help. And he was beginning to miss his home.

One day he'd been painting an English house to earn some money. The house was just a half mile or so from his folks' place. Nora believes the daily trips over to paint near his old home worked on him a little, perhaps evoking a bit of homesickness. Nora mentioned to Jonas that she needed eggs and thought maybe they could stop by his folks' place to buy some. If he didn't feel comfortable, she told him, she'd pick up eggs at the store instead. Jonas told her he wanted to have her buy them from his folks.

So early on a Saturday afternoon in March, a year and two months after he left, Jonas let Nora drive him over in her truck. Jonas had been worrying more and more about being deported to Canada. Every chance he got, his ex-Amish friend Noah joked that he was going to call the police and have Jonas deported. Now that he had turned down Keim's help, Jonas needed his father to sign an affidavit stating that he had lived in the States for the required years. Jonas also knew there was a good chance his father would refuse to sign the affidavit, believing that by not signing it he had a better chance of thwarting Jonas's plans to leave Amish life for good, which would make it easier for Jonas to give up, return home, get baptized, and get on with the business of being a member in good standing of the Swartzentruber Amish, where he belonged.

An ex-Swartzentruber Amish woman from Kentucky who's been living with the Keims has had the support of her parents in a way Jonas has not. "I can't complain about my parents," Barbara says. "They've always been good to me. I know my parents would like it if I came home. It's hard on them, but my dad [who is a bishop] was always like 'everybody gets to choose how they want to live.' We've been writing letters back and forth. He never mentions me leaving, but he always ends with a little scripture."

Jonas would not be as lucky. When Nora and Jonas pulled into the driveway that cold Saturday afternoon, they spotted several of Jonas's younger siblings playing in the yard. Ordinarily the kids swarmed the truck, but on this day they were watchful and kept their distance. Jonas's kid brother, Harvey, who's the oldest boy in the family now that Jonas has left, brushed by Jonas as if he weren't there at all, and a couple of Jonas's younger sisters followed suit.

Another of Jonas's sisters came out of the house and greeted Jonas, and he told her he wanted to buy some eggs. Then in a burst, four of Jonas's little brothers rushed up to him, tugging at his clothes, seeming to be delighted by their eldest brother's visit. As Nora sat in the truck and Jonas joshed with his little brothers, his mother looked out the kitchen window. Nora decided to stay in the truck and out of the way to give Jonas and his family whatever time and privacy they needed.

A minute or two later, Menno came out of the house looking groggy, as if he might have been sleeping, although he usually works on Saturday. He immediately sent Jonas's brothers back into the house and he and Jonas began to talk. Five minutes passed. And then ten. Nora thought Jonas looked upset; the talk didn't seem to be going well. After fifteen minutes Nora rolled down her window in hopes of distracting Menno with polite conversation as a way of easing the tension.

She called Menno's name three times before he acknowledged her. She asked him if he might not want the waste manure from her farm. Menno told her that he could use it but he couldn't haul it. Nora told him she could do the hauling.

He shrugged his shoulders and resumed talking to Jonas.

Nora rolled up her window and resumed her wait. As she looked around, she spied two of Jonas's little sisters crouched covertly beneath the windowsill.

Ann, Jonas's mother, came out of the house then and walked to the storage unit behind the house. When she finished with the storage unit and was headed back to the house, she turned around and looked directly at Jonas, but she didn't say a word. After she went back inside, she and another daughter watched Jonas and Menno out of the kitchen window. Soon another face peered out the window in the mudroom, and two more gazed out the window of an upstairs bedroom.

All girls, all watching, Nora thought, feeling as if she were about to cry. She could tell from Jonas's face that whatever his father was telling him was making him angry. Nora thought that if Jonas only glanced around the windows of his home at the aching faces of his sisters and mother, he would see how much he was loved. She couldn't help thinking what a shame it was that as family-oriented as the Amish are believed to be, on this late-winter afternoon none of them truly had the freedom to show that they loved their brother, their son.

Nora found out later that Jonas's anger on that day rose out of the fact that Menno told him, and not for the first time, that not only would Jonas be going to hell for joining the English world and leaving the Amish one behind, but that his parents would also burn in hell for Jonas's sin. When Jonas questioned his father as to the source of this information, he was told that according to one minister Menno had spoken with, a child's leaving the Amish meant that the parents were not doing their job properly. He was causing trouble for the whole family. I can imagine Jonas shifting his gaze from the ground to his father's face and back as he challenged what he considered a dubious point of theology by telling his father how stupid that idea was. He also challenged Menno or any other Amish person to find that in the Bible. Menno admitted that the minister was Levi's brother. (Levi was the neighbor who had given Jonas a hard time when he first tried to leave.) Jonas later confided to Nora that Levi and his brother haunted him. Jonas was afraid of Levi's brother, believing that the man was always trying to get him in trouble even before he'd left the Amish life.

Jonas went on to tell his dad that it was time he got some guts and stood up for himself and his family. I can imagine Jonas now, facing his dad, taking his hands out of the pocket of his jeans jacket, saying what he had to say loudly enough so it could be heard by his siblings. He said he was tired of all the gossip and that after being away he could see how gossiping was tearing up the Amish community. He again demanded to know where the Bible said a parent should disown his child. Jonas told Menno that it was his choice and nobody else's not to let him back into the family home. He went on to tell his dad that he felt unloved and unwanted.

Apparently Nora had misinterpreted the actions of Jonas's little brothers when they had jumped around him and tugged and poked at his clothes. Jonas later said that his brothers were telling him how bad his English clothes were, and that they laughed at the slight tear in his work jacket.

Trying to reach out to his father, Jonas told Menno that he would pay to have his dirt driveway graveled, but Menno refused his offer, telling him that he had caused enough trouble. Jonas then offered to go to see the bishop in person and explain that his leaving had nothing to do with his parents and was nobody else's business but his. Menno again accused Jonas of leaving the Amish to be with Kathleen and claimed that she was taking all of his money. Jonas tried to explain that the Gilberts were taking nothing from him, but Menno would not hear it.

Nora finally rolled down the window and hollered out to Jonas that they had to get going because Kathleen and her toddler son were sick at home. Nora saw a look of relief on Jonas's face, and he later thanked her for giving him an excuse to leave.

After this visit, Jonas became more adamant that he would never go back. "I can't believe I used to live that way. It's so dirty," Jonas said. Nora wished she could help his parents understand that she and her family were not the enemy. She had thought they'd be happy knowing that their son was safe. She had hoped Menno and Ann could sit down and have a civil, honest conversation with their son, but now she felt that would not happen. She admitted her admiration and respect for certain aspects of Amish life have soured. As we sat in her front room, Nora became animated, moving up in her chair. Her voice was raised. She now believes that Amish life prevents parents from getting to really know their children—that they do not communicate with them, that the life prevents them from helping their kids solve their problems. Because of the isolation Jonas felt, he saw himself as alone, realizing he would have to solve his problems.

"It's just what I thought it would be. People had come from the church and told my dad I was going to hell. And then he told me not to come around the house or talk to my sisters or brothers. I thought they were going to come for me. They were going to come for me, but they came for Ann instead," Jonas said. His sister Ann was baptized soon after this visit, and Jonas believes it was church pressure on his parents that hurried her into baptism.

I sometimes had the feeling that Nora was enjoying her role

as Jonas's surrogate mother just a little too much, and that she welcomed giving voice to her fresh insights into Amish life. She often predicted I'd have trouble with Samuel if he read the book. She told me our friendship could never survive the telling of this story, just as hers with Menno could not survive Jonas's leaving.

I hope I'm never faced with the situation Nora faced. What would I do if one of Samuel's children, say Rebekah, for instance, came to our house and said she wanted to leave the Amish and wanted us to help her? I imagine her standing on our front porch in the middle of the night, lonely and frightened and cold, desperate and in need. If she were fourteen, fifteen, sixteen years old, my wife and I would take her right back to her parents. But what if she came to us at eighteen, nineteen, twenty, as an adult, an adult with free will and the desire to live her one precious life exactly as she wanted to live it? Would I remind her of the beauty and goodness in a Swartzentruber Amish life? Would I tell her she'd never again know the security of community the way she knows it now? Would I help her turn her back on that community and on that beauty and goodness? Choosing to help Rebekah could mean losing her parents as friends, causing them immense pain, thwarting their efforts to hold her. Not helping her would be turning our backs on a young woman who believed she needed our help to make the biggest decision of her young life, a young woman who had trusted and liked us for years, a young woman we'd be saying no to. Samuel and Mary, because of who they are as people and parents, have children I care for as individuals. Rebekah is not only the daughter of Samuel and Mary Shetler. She is also Rebekah Shetler, and I know my family and I would do anything for any member of the Shetler family.

I pray we're never forced to make a decision like this. By praying for that, I'm not exactly sure what I mean: That she stays a Swartzentruber Amish? That she stays Amish only if it's what she wants to do? That she leaves and keeps us out of it?

Maybe I just don't have the guts to answer my own questions.

SEVEN

The Lot Falls

Hank the dog, who's had a recent run-in with a skunk, greets me on the road before I even arrive at the Shetlers' place to visit. I return Hank's greeting with words only, figuring I'll make it up to him when the skunk's nothing more than a distant memory. I walk up the driveway and wave to Samuel, who's just come out on the porch. Actually, "driveway" sounds a bit generous in this case. In front of the produce stand, Samuel and Mary have covered the dirt and mud with shredded shingles. A sprinkle of gravel greets buggies and cars coming onto the driveway, but it soon gives way to dirt on dry days and mud when it rains: a Swartzentruber driveway. The shingles and gravel are a concession Samuel has made for his English produce customers. He's filling up a water jug, while Rebekah sweeps off the debris of the night. The trailer door is wide open, as it usually is. I'd mentioned to Samuel that I'd be coming by at seven our time, six his. "I'll be a few minutes yet," he says. I know this about Samuel: He's always running behind because he's always running. "I've had my breakfast, but I still have to say the morning prayer." He walks back inside, closing the door behind him. I stay on the porch.

For the last six months, the family has been living in a

trailer, converted to an Amish home. Samuel originally bought
the trailer with the intention of expanding the produce stand
and converting the rest of the trailer into a workshop, where he
plans to make furniture. Instead, they decided to build a new
house, a house suitable for eleven people, so in one day, they
and their Amish friends and neighbors tore down the house to
the stone foundation on which they'll build their new house.
The trailer has become a temporary miniature version of their
home. Two bedrooms separated by hanging blankets divide the
back of the trailer in half—one side for the parents, the other
for the boys. The girls sleep upstairs in the dawdy haus (grandfather house), which is where their grandparents live. There's
also a single bed in the kitchen area, just as there was in the old
house and just like there will be in the new one. The Swartzentruber Amish are forbidden any stuffed chairs or couches; all
the chairs are wood, so the single bed makes for a soft place to
sit when it's not being used as a bed by the youngest kids. I've
learned that there's no use asking Samuel and Mary why they're
not allowed to have couches and stuffed chairs. Their answer
will be a smile, a slight shoulder shrug, and "That's just the way
it is." I have no doubt the restriction has to do with the idle
hands and the devil's workshop philosophy. I also know that
my leather couch and recliner beckon me in ways my oak
kitchen chairs do not.

The Shetler kitchen is composed of a black wood-burning
stove, which heats the house and cooks the food. Wooden
homemade cupboards and counters run along one wall. There's
a long wooden table and chairs. The walls are white and uncov-
ered, and the molding is simple pine painted dark blue. There
is no wallpaper, no decorative knickknacks, no paintings or

prints. Only a clock and a calendar hang on the kitchen walls. The calendar is from a feed shop and comes without monthly pictures. One can hear the tick of the thirty-day clock keeping Swartzentruber Amish time, which ignores daylight savings. The more modern Old Order Amish of surrounding counties adhere to daylight savings. Because so few of the Old Order Amish work on farms anymore, and instead most have stores and shops in towns, they've accepted daylight savings in order to be in synch with customers and other store owners. The Swartzentruber Amish remain fixed, approximately 150 years "behind" us. And for seven months of the year, they're 150 years and one hour behind.

For as long as I've known him, Samuel has dreamed of moving west, to Iowa or Missouri, where two of his brothers and one sister have moved in the past few years. They moved for several reasons, not the least of which were fewer people and cheaper land. Samuel still itches to move, but he faces obstacles. Mary has her family only a couple of miles away and wants to stay in Ohio. Although there is no doubt that the Swartzentruber Amish order is an unadulterated patriarchy, Samuel's main reason for not having moved already is because his wife doesn't want to move. Complicating things further is Mary's father. Mary's father, Jonathan, lent Samuel some of the money that allowed him to buy his eighty-six-acre farm. Recently, even though Mary is steadfastly against moving, Samuel and his father went to sound Jonathan out about hypothetically working out a deal on the land if the family were Iowa bound. Jonathan wouldn't even entertain the notion. But Samuel still aches.

Samuel and I often talk about being in similar positions. We both want to move to the West, but our wives do not.

Commiserating is one avenue of conversation for us. Samuel would like to move the family to Iowa, following in his brother's footsteps. In Iowa somebody can buy twice as much land for the same money you'd spend here. Plus the soil is better and there aren't as many people—meaning there aren't as many cars on the roads. One of Samuel's sisters and two of his brothers moved out to Iowa and western Missouri in the past few years.

"He's living where I want to be living," Samuel says of his brother. "Sometimes when I think of all this work, and all we do is fertilize it so it will all grow again . . ." His voice trails off.

Amish farmers in Iowa and western Missouri raise mostly beef. Because of the less severe winters, there's grazing on grass all year round. One brother has 190 acres (at $550 an acre, without buildings) and another brother has nearly as many, which he bought for $1,550 an acre including buildings. Samuel's brother John is about to move out to the place he just bought in western Missouri. "So he's going to see a change in his life," Samuel says. "He's in for a real adventure."

I know Samuel wishes he could make this same move. His brother in Iowa raises thirty-five cows, no milk, just meat. This means he does not have to farm as much as Samuel; nor does he have to raise chickens and ducks, run a produce stand, raise bees and turkeys, and operate a woodshop on the side.

If Samuel moved to Iowa, all he'd have to do is keep thirty-five cattle healthy, sell them for meat once a year, and piddle in his workshop making furniture, which is something he likes to do if he can ever find the time.

But for now he'll settle for a new home.

→ ←

Hummingbirds flutter manically around the hanging baskets of petunias for sale as I wait for Samuel on the front porch. I kill time counting and recounting the turkeys, all white, lounging around a penned area. I know that Samuel and Mary bought twenty young birds, but as many times as I count them, there appear to be only sixteen. As I count I remember a character in Margaret Atwood's novel *Cat's Eye* referring to a turkey dinner as "eating lost flight." I continue counting lost flight while I wait. Later on Samuel informs me that four of his turkeys died this year, where last year all survived until they could be sold for Thanksgiving.

Seven bags of corncobs hang in bags outside the wash house. Behind me nine pairs of rubber boots stand sentry. One pair, belonging to eight-year-old Andy, has a few holes. These holes have caused Andy and his family some unpleasantness lately. "The girls were saying that the hog pens were bursting with manure," Mary told me. It was Andy's job to clean them out. Andy is stockier than his father and brothers. He seems to love to eat, play, and work in equal measure, although not even Andy enjoys mucking out the hog pens. Although I concede there's a certain aromatic pleasantness to horse manure, hog manure offers the nose nothing but stench. The girls kicked their brother out of the trailer when he walked into the kitchen, without his boots but still in his socks, which, because of his perforated boots, were thick with hog waste. A small table with washbasins sits to the side of the line of boots. Since the family has been living in the trailer, they have had to wash up outside. There's also an old metal filing cabinet with a variety of buckets on top. A gnomelike plastic owl given to Esther by an English guy sits perched on the table. A fledgling English walnut tree

grows in front of the horseshoe driveway just south of the produce stand, and beyond it is another garden, about the size of a
suburban front lawn, where the family grows cabbage, red
beets, flowers, and broccoli. The front porch looks out over a
deep field of wheat that ends in trees and woods for as far as I
can see.

Samuel comes back out about fifteen minutes later. When
he does he turns his back to me slightly, removes his false teeth,
and washes them out with water from the basin on the table, on
the porch. He's had false teeth since his early thirties. The
Amish I know use toothpastes with fluoride, so their teeth
should be as healthy as anyone else's, but getting false teeth is
often a financial decision. Rather than pay to see a dentist for
each toothache or cavity for the rest of their lives, they pay once
to have their teeth removed and dentures put in. Samuel and
Mary don't like to talk much about their "dentist." "We don't
want to get anybody in trouble," Mary says. As far as I can tell,
the "dentist" is an Amish man with a hidden and marketable
vocation, or an English chiropractor who does dental work, il-
legally, on the side. English professionals in the area have been
known to help the Amish when it comes to keeping health-care
costs down. While running a table saw to help with the building of the new house, Rebekah got hit with a piece of hickory
that kicked out of the blade and slammed into her face. She
cried and screamed as blood poured down her face, chest, and
arms. Everybody feared missing fingers or damaged eyes. Luckily, the wood missed her eye, hitting her on the cheekbone and
the forehead. The nearest hospital was over fifteen miles away.
Because only Amish were at the farm that day, there was no

phone to call 911. Samuel could have run from English house to English house hoping like hell somebody was home and then asking the English to call 911. Instead, he carried her to the buggy, rein-slapped the horse, and rushed his bleeding daughter—to a nearby veterinarian. The vet checked Rebekah out and told Samuel to watch for signs of concussion. He then stitched her up for free. A couple of weeks later, Rebekah pulled out the stitches herself.

→ ←

I shadow Samuel, following close behind as he goes about a few chores. His brain, feeding off his senses, seems to be going all the time, mostly casting around the farm for things to tell me or to remind himself about. He points to the nest of a barn swallow, which is stuck to the side of a beam above the horse stalls in the barn. "Growing up in Canada, we had eave swallows, and at one time there were over three hundred nests along the side of the barn," he says. The amateur ornithologist then explains that eave swallows are similar to barn swallows but they don't have the split in the tail feathers that marks a barn swallow; and then he tells me that honeybees live for only six weeks. We walk into a chicken coop that's big enough, as my dad would say, for a young couple to fix up and move into as a first home. Three hundred chicks reside in a twelve-by-eight shed. Samuel raises Ancona chicks, multicolored browns and tans. These lay blue-and-green eggs; the younger and smaller chicks live in a loft inside the shed. Another shed, with a cement floor that used to be for the pigs, is filled with Black Australorps, an Australian breed known for laying a slew of eggs. Samuel gets fresh water for the hundreds of chicks. The odor coming from the Ancona camp is precisely what you'd expect three hundred cooped up, shittin' chickens to smell like. No more. And certainly no less.

Just south of the two coops are three hogs. One huge hog has ears as big as a good-sized rabbit's. He's stretched out in a pool of muddy water. We make our way to the barn, which Samuel added to a few years ago to make more box stalls. Now one section of the barn has four stalls and two water troughs on the east wall, and one box stall and four other regular stalls across the packed dirt-and-straw floor. At any time the stalls could shelter cows, horses, ducks, newborn calves, and goats. Ben and Bill stand in two adjoining stalls. Ben, a six-year-old mare, has run off a few times. The first time she took off was also the first time she was hitched up to the spreader with Bill, her brother. A kid, thirteen or fourteen, who was helping Samuel jumped off a high pile of haystacks, and Ben and Bill bolted and jumped a fence—"like leap frogs," Samuel said. "The horses ran around like they were having a parade, their tails higher than their heads." Now both horses have to wear leather hoods when they're out pulling a wagon or plow. The outside world just does something to them. According to Samuel, Ben and Bill's mother was a little crazy too.

As we walk around the barn, I ask Samuel about the morning prayer that had held him up earlier. He tells me it's one he reads every dawn except Sunday, when he offers a special prayer. The daily Old German prayer usually takes from five to seven minutes to say, giving thanks to God for a restful night and asking his guidance and protection in the day ahead.

Samuel is committed beyond all else to his church and his role in it, and he has good reason to be: God chose Samuel just before Halloween of 2004, the day he became a minister.

Every church district or group has one bishop, two ministers, and a deacon. (A bishop may be the head of two small districts.) For several years now Samuel has been a deacon. Until his group ordains a new deacon, Samuel's a minister and a deacon. Only the bishop can marry or bury anybody. He baptizes the flock. He excommunicates the wayward. He leads the shunning that follows excommunication. Under him are two ministers, whose job is to do much of the preaching on Sundays and to be responsible for the material welfare of the community. And beneath the ministers is a deacon who works closely with the bishop to keep the sheep from straying. For days before Samuel's first time preaching at the fall church council, he'd spent hours reading and memorizing parts of the Bible. No notes are allowed to be used. No sermons are written in advance. For three hours the minister preaches from memory and out of devotion. Unlike non-Amish ministers, who choose their calling, most Amish men—at least the Amish men I know best—hope beyond hope they will not be called, that the lot will not fall on them. If it does, the minister is a minister for life. The job comes without pay but with many responsibilities, serious ones. All the preparation that goes into the position is done on top of farming and family. The last thing Samuel wanted was to become minister, but he was chosen, so he has to serve.

The big day for Samuel occurred at the communion, which is held by the Amish twice a year, in the fall and the spring.

Samuel admits to having no idea that Jacob Ammann, for whom the Amish are named, instituted communion twice yearly instead of just yearly, which was the standard practice of other Anabaptists. However, regardless of when it was instituted or by whom, Samuel's glad they do it twice a year for practical reasons. Sometimes a man might be sick, or a woman pregnant, due any day and not able to be at the communion. Instead of missing a whole year, he or she can catch the next communion. There's another practical reason. At the church council, which is held two weeks before the communion is scheduled, the baptized men and women of the church—no children or unbaptized teens allowed—come together to make sure everybody is in agreement with the Ordnung. The men and women will be segregated with one minister polling every man and one every woman, asking if he or she agrees to the Ordnung. The pressure to conform must be intense. Samuel can recall no woman ever announcing her opposition to any part of the Ordnung. Any baptized members who have a problem with the church rules must stand up in front of the members of their district and speak their mind. Unless a problem can be resolved right then and there, the communion service is postponed and cannot be held until everything is worked out. "Somebody could stand up and say that he wants rubber tires on his buggy. If he won't come around to the church's way of thinking, we won't be able to have communion," Samuel says. He also says that rubber tires would be a deal breaker. It will never happen. Not among the Swartzentrubers of Ashland County. In a case like this, a person would split off and form another church group whose Ordnung would permit rubber tires instead of the steel tires on Samuel's church's buggies. "I've always thought you should draw the line and then keep it there. If you start changing it, the line keeps moving." Also, anybody who has been in violation of the Ordnung—and, theoretically, it could be anyone from somebody caught using a chainsaw to somebody seen driving a car to somebody committing adultery—has to confess his or her transgression in front of the entire congregation. If, however, there are no overt problems, the district can proceed with its communion two weeks hence.

And so it was when Samuel became minister. Any married, baptized man is eligible to be ordained. Two weeks before the communion, at the council meeting, the whole church will give its approval for the need to appoint a minister at the upcoming communion. First there will be a communion service and the foot washing. The members will break homemade bread and take a sip of wine. (Making the wine is the deacon's job.) After the breaking of bread, men will wash the feet of other men and women the feet of women, until all members of the church have had their feet cleaned, following the example and teachings of Jesus as described in the book of John: "After that he poureth water into a bason [sic], and began to wash the disciples' feet, and to wipe them with the towel wherewith he was girded" (13:5) and "If I then, your Lord and Master, have washed your feet; ye also ought to wash one another's feet" (13:14). Before the nomination there will be a meal. When it's time to choose a new bishop, minister (preacher), or deacon, men and women will make nominations.

Among the Swartzentrubers, a current minister will stand inside the house next to an open window, while on the outside, first the men, then the women file by and speak the name of a man they'd like to see become minister. A current minister then writes down the names. When the voting is finished, everybody comes back inside the house. Before the names of the lot are read, the congregation comes together in a silent prayer. Then the bishop announces "how many brothers there are in the lot." "Everybody shrinks about an inch when they hear their name," Samuel says. Because Samuel received two or more nominations, he and seven other men became brothers in the lot. This was Samuel's fourth lot. His third lot made him a deacon. The bishop then prepares the hymnbooks. He slips a note in one of the books, ties each book shut with a piece of string and lays them on the table up front, which is usually where the oldest men in the church sit. Once the bishop has the books on the table, explains Samuel, "a minister comes and messes it for him [shuffles the books], so even he doesn't know where it is." It was at this point that Samuel was praying he'd be spared, saying over and over again, "Surely not me. Surely not me." And this was not false modesty. Although all Amish men will accept this lot if it falls to them, hardly any man desires it. The biblical undergirding for this casting of lots appears in Proverbs 6:33, which reads, "The lot is cast into the lap; but the whole disposing thereof is of the Lord," and Acts 1:24 and 26, in which Matthias is chosen to replace Judas ("And they prayed, and said, Thou, Lord, which knowest the hearts of all men, shew whether of these two thou hast chosen . . . And they gave forth their lots; and the lot fell upon Matthias; and he was numbered with the eleven apostles").

Samuel stood in line with the other seven men. Eight hymnbooks—tied shut with string and shuffled so even the bishop wouldn't know which book held the lot—sat on a nearby table. The candidates then walked to the table and chose a book. In one of these hymnbooks was a scrap of paper that read, simply, "You are chosen." And then the bishop approached the brother closest to him and snapped the string. "It's so quiet," Samuel says. "The snap of the string is the only sound in the room." By the time he got to Samuel, the bishop had snapped the string on four books and hadn't found the piece of paper. When it was Samuel's turn, the bishop snapped the string and opened the book. He found the scrap of paper that held a man's fate. The lot had fallen on Samuel. God had chosen him to be a minister. "I didn't want to be a minister," Samuel says. "But God chose me, so I have to be." After Samuel was chosen, he stepped to the center of the room where the ordained men sat. The new minister and the bishop stood facing one another, and the bishop read from the New Testament. (When a bishop is chosen, two bishops from other districts must be present, and the newly ordained will kneel in front of a bishop.) "Basically, I was told that as minister I had to work to hinder the bad and fertilize the good." On that day, Samuel became a minister for life. Samuel prays he'll never become a bishop, whose job is also for life. He considers himself lucky that his bishop is only a year older than he is, and he wishes the man a long life. "Hearts are very soft when somebody is chosen," Samuel says. "It's not uncommon to hear people crying. The new minister's wife might be crying. Other people's hearts might be soft because they're remembering times in the past when somebody was chosen." The day ended with the evening prayer, just the way all Swartzentruber church days end.

When I learned of Samuel's becoming minister, he was in

front of his house dressing turkeys for English people who had placed their orders for Thanksgiving birds. (The Amish I know don't have a huge holiday feast for Thanksgiving, although they are well aware that the English do, so turkeys and pumpkin pie will be available for sale.) It was clear his new vocation lay heavily on him. When he told me about having been chosen, he spoke with the voice of a tired man, of a man carrying a fresh and onerous burden. As I've said before, there is not enough daylight or time in a Samuel Shetler day to accomplish everything he strives to do. And now there was this—chosen by God as the second-highest authority in his church. And it was not just added responsibility for Samuel. Mary was now a minister's wife and the children a minister's children. They would be expected to live exemplary Swartzentruber Amish lives.

Beyond—or beneath—Samuel's official status as a minister in his church lies his personal faith. Samuel's faith is strong and absolute. He believes that God created the world in six days, and that Adam and Eve were flesh-and-blood human beings who were "seduced by the subtlety and deceit of the serpent," thus bringing sin and death into the world. Samuel also believes in a literal heaven and hell, the Virgin Birth, and the resurrection of the body. As noted Amish scholar John A. Hostetler has written: "Through the Fall man became heir to a disobedient and carnal nature. Redemption is made possible by responding to God's love. The Amish believe they are recipients of an undeserved gift—thus they live in a moral predicament; for they must prove worthy, faithful, grateful, and humble. God's gift obligates the Amish to reciprocate, by offering in return a community permeated with the attributes of Christ: walking in righteousness, sacrificial suffering, obedience, submission, humility, and nonresistance."

Although the central document of Samuel's faith, the Dordrecht Confession, created at a Dutch Mennonite meeting in 1632, is almost four hundred years old, it's present in the way Samuel lives his life in the twenty-first century. The Dordrecht Confession was shaped by the Schleitheim Articles of 1527, whose first tenet is adult baptism, a founding credo of Anabaptist life then and now. The second and third tenets have to do with keeping the body of believers pure and together. The "ban," or shunning, is no doubt the most well-known of Amish practices, and the articles are specific regarding this practice: "if any inadvertently slip and fall into error and sin, the ban shall be employed. First they will be warned twice privately"—which is Samuel's job as the deacon—"and the third time publicly before the congregation." Remaining separate from the wickedness of the world, "which the devil has planted," is commanded by the fourth article. The fifth expresses the Anabaptist belief in local rule, where the shepherd is chosen by the flock, which is why Samuel's being a deacon and a minister brings with it heavy responsibility. And the sixth, my personal favorite, states that the sword and its violence belong to governments, and are "outside the perfection of Christ." This tenet recognizes that "the rule of government is according to the flesh; that of Christians, according to the spirit." The articles end with language forbidding the swearing of oaths. One hundred years later the eighteen tenets of the Dordrecht Confession of Faith augmented the Schleitheim Articles. Although Samuel knows the tenets well, he knows nothing of their origin.

→ ←

As much as I have derided other people, including other writers, for their appropriation of the Amish for their own needs, I too have sought out Samuel at times, times when I needed sustenance.

Last Sunday, while riding my bike down County Road 281, I came up behind a buggy heading to church. As I got close to the buggy I saw that two toddlers, a boy around two and a girl maybe a year older, were standing up in back. Because it was a warm summer morning, the buggy's back flap was open. Two bungee cords forming an X were hooked up as a way of keeping the kids safe. Pedaling faster now and wanting to pass the buggy, I glanced behind me to check for cars. Then I heard a thump and a scream. The little boy had fallen from the back of the buggy. His father, a young man in his early twenties, stopped the horse, jumped out, walked around back, and picked up his son.

"I couldn't tell if he hit his head," I said. "Is he okay?"

"I don't think he hit his head," the boy's father said, no doubt trying to convince himself with his words.

The man ran his hand lightly over the boy's blond hair, checking for bumps and scrapes, and then he carried him to the buggy and headed off without saying another word to me.

Three days later, on a Wednesday, I was cycling down the same road when I saw upwards of eighty buggies parked on a farm. It wasn't an auction, and it couldn't be a wedding because they almost always happened on Thursdays in the fall. It had to be a funeral. Immediately I thought about the little boy.

I hurried over to Samuel's farm and found him perched on top of fifteen feet of hay on a wagon pulled by two plow horses. Barely visible in the mountain of hay sat Andy, who on this afternoon was in charge of controlling the horses. One false or too-fast move by the horses and Andy's father would fall a couple of stories. The goal was to get the hay spread out to use for mulch before the rain came. Samuel has a farmer's sense of when rain is coming, and he seems to know as much from experience and empirical evidence as the Weather Channel deduces with its Doppler technology. The barn was already full and this hay too wet for anything more useful than mulch. Samuel threw a heaping pitchfork full of hay to the ground, and then Lena and Rebekah spread it around.

"I see there's a funeral over on 281," I said.

"Yeah. I stopped by on Monday to see him. I was told there would be plenty of people from his district going to the funeral, so since he wasn't family I stayed home."

"Who was it that died?"

Please don't let it be the little boy.

"Choe Keim. He slept in and was hit by a car," Samuel said.

The little boy was alive.

By "slept in" Samuel meant Keim—no relation to Joe Keim of MAP—fell asleep while driving his buggy, which is something that happens a lot. Samuel has admitted to falling asleep at the reins, but only for seconds at a time. Not long ago I saw a horse pulling a hack behind it at ten thirty at night. When I saw only a blanket on the seat I thought maybe a little kid had "slept in" and the horse was taking him home. I was almost right. Samuel told me that his brother-in-law's horse had taken off after an auction and cantered all the way home in the dark without lit lanterns, going south on State Route 301 and then turning right and heading south on State Route 42, and then home. Neither Keim nor his horse was this lucky.

At around ten o'clock Saturday night, Keim and his two teenage daughters were driving home from selling baked goods at a Saturday farmer's market. The drive home takes several hours. Keim and his daughters fell asleep, and the horse went past a stop sign and out onto the road. The seventeen-year-old kid driving the car hit the buggy broadside. Rescue workers pronounced Keim dead at the scene. His two daughters were released from the hospital the next day with only minor injuries. The horse had a broken hind leg and had to be put down.

"God must have wanted him," Samuel said. "Just think, if it would have been thirty seconds later, he might have woken up. He had seventeen kids, and only one was married."

"How old was he?"

"Forty-seven or -eight."

"Why do you think it was God's will for a forty-seven-year-old man with seventeen kids to be killed?" I asked. As soon as the words left my mouth, I regretted having said them.

Samuel threw another pitchfork of hay down off the wagon. "I guess his work on this earth was done," Samuel said, having taken no ostensible offense at my question.

I know Samuel does not throw the words "God's will" around the way I've heard some other believers say them. Usually when I hear these words, the person saying them appears to be figuratively throwing up his or her hands, almost as if there's really no sense in grieving for somebody when the tragedy was all part of God's plan. But that's not how I take it when it comes from Samuel. The man knows heartache. He's buried his first-born child. He talks about God's will the way he reports how much it rained the night before or that one of his cows has the milk disease. God's will is like gravity—it is rain and dirt and sun and snow and wind and fire and every other elemental thing. It is what it is—no matter what we do.

As much as my defenses go up when I hear people explain life's tragedies away as God's will, I have sought Samuel out at times of personal sorrow. A couple of days after an uncle of mine died last spring, I walked up to the farm to let Samuel know. He and my uncle had known each other in a casual way, but Samuel hadn't yet been told of his death.

I noticed that somebody had dropped off an old refrigerator. A lot of Samuel's English neighbors give him whatever they believe is broken down or used up, including scrap wood and old chicken wire. No matter what it is, they believe Samuel will find a use for it. Samuel will use the old fridge for storage. "There's another one behind the woodshed," he said. "When we butcher cows or hogs we'll put the meat in there so the dog or cats won't get at it. In winter it will freeze. Sometimes we pack it with ice."

Samuel also has one of the most unlikely things you'd ever think to find on an Amish farm. Inside the backyard-size chicken-wired pen that cages seventy-odd ducks sits a luggage carrier from Continental Airlines given to Samuel by an English guy who works for the airline. Samuel uses it to store kerosene.

After we discussed refrigerators that will never function as refrigerators, I told him about Uncle Bob. "I just wanted you to know," I said.

"He was always nice when he came here," Samuel said. "The girls really liked him. Apple butter and eggs seemed to be all he ever wanted. He must have loved apple butter."

Samuel paused for a few seconds and then asked what I guessed he'd been wanting to ask for a long time.

"What exactly was wrong with Uncle Bob?"

I explained that a tumor was discovered on the frontal lobe of his brain when he was a year old. The plan was to use radiation to remove the tumor. Because radiation use was relatively new in the 1930s, the doctors used too much of it, or used it for too long a time (the family's never been sure and has never tried to find out), and part of Uncle Bob's brain was damaged. Because of this, he couldn't read, do simple math, drive a car, marry, or support himself. But he could be everybody's friend, and be the lucky owner of an endless spirit.

"Some doctor just screwed up," I said, feeling angry about a man's damaged life and fresh death.

"Maybe a doctor made a mistake, but God didn't," Samuel said. "God made Uncle Bob that way because everybody who knew him needed him to be exactly the way he was."

Everybody who knew him needed him to be exactly the way he was. These words opened up new thought trails in my mind. Over five hundred people attended Uncle Bob's funeral, making it clear that he knew and was known by people the rest of us saw only as strangers, strangers who sobbed for a man with a victimized brain and a damaged heart. *Everybody who knew him needed him to be exactly the way he was.* With Samuel's words in my head, I decided—almost unconsciously—not to engage him in a philosophical discussion where I play the grieved and skeptical infidel and he the faithful and steadfast pilgrim. What I did instead was let his words soak in. And pretty soon I was not as angry, and even a little less sad. I knew Samuel said what he did not to make me feel better or seize the opportunity to evangelize, which is not the Amish way. He said it because he believes it, from the brim of his straw hat right down to the bottom of his rubber boots. As much as I cannot allow or force myself to believe in fate and God in quite the same way Samuel does, I was comforted by his words.

Instead of fighting the usual intellectual battles with myself or with Samuel, I simply gave myself to the moment, allowing Samuel's philosophy to be mine for as long as I stayed on the farm.

I stayed for much of the afternoon.

EIGHT

The Amish FBI

Lately I've been hearing rumors about Jonas. Because we haven't been in touch much, he has begun to be suspicious of me. I heard from Kathleen that Jonas suspects I'm not writing a book at all. He believes that because Samuel and I are friends, the writing of the book was part of some elaborate ruse, a conspiracy. Jonas believes I'm working in concert with Samuel and the church to force him to return to the fold. Jonas does not return my calls and never answers his cell when he sees my number in its screen.

Having grown up in the most conservative order of a conservative people, an order where community is intense and suspicion about the outside world immense, Jonas is willing to believe just about anything, especially about the English world. There's no doubt that all the Amish I know best have deep suspicions and biases concerning the "sinful world" the non-Amish inhabit. No matter how many people tell Jonas it's not true, he's convinced there is an Amish FBI. He's heard this special bureau consists of retired FBI agents who have been hired by the Amish to spy on their children. When Jonas worked for an English farmer before leaving the Amish, the farmer would encourage him to wear English clothes and to ride his four-wheeler, which Jonas gladly did. Returning home one day after burning up a field in the four-wheeler, Jonas was confronted by his parents, who said they had pictures of Jonas dressed as an English person and riding a four-wheeler. Jonas was convinced the agents of the Amish FBI had been conducting surveillance on him, taking pictures of his wayward behavior and presenting the evidence to his parents.

Kathleen is the key to convincing Jonas that I am writing a book, and that I'm not a secret agent for his church. I meet her for a talk at a local dive on a stifling hot July day. She orders ice tea and later a scoop of ice cream.

"Does Jonas really believe there's not a book?" I ask.

"Yes. He says he talked to somebody who knows you and that person didn't know anything about a book."

Jonas, who can do almost anything when it comes to construction, had been putting up drywall for an acquaintance of ours who was building a new house. Jonas couldn't believe that she didn't know about the book, which struck me as bizarre until I recalled how the Swartzentruber Amish community Jonas was reared in seems to know nearly every move anybody makes.

"What can I do to assure him that I'm not working with the Amish to make him go back?"

"I'll talk to him."

As she's nearing the end of her ice cream, Kathleen's cell phone rings. It's Jonas. She tells him she's here with me and that she believes that I am indeed writing a book. Jonas agrees to start answering my calls.

I have to wonder what goes through Jonas's head. Why would he think some non-Amish guy was deceiving him about writing a book just to trick him into going home? Joe Keim, the ex-Amish founder of MAP, believes that most Amish, maybe all, and especially the most conservative and restricted, live double lives: a life they show other Amish and the church, and the life they lead when nobody else is around. So why should the English be any different? "From the bishop on down, it's 'as long as I don't get caught [by the church] it's okay.'"

I believe I can pinpoint the day Jonas began getting suspicious of me. One day late last winter, Samuel asked me how many Amish people I'd mentioned the book to. I told him I hadn't told a single Amish person—that as far as the Amish were concerned, he and his family were the only people who knew. This had been part of our agreement. I assured him again that I had told no other Amish.

"The reason I ask is because Jonas's father came to me and said that he'd heard I was telling an English guy all about our church for a book he's writing," Samuel said. "I think Jonas must have said something to him."

Menno was referring to the day Nora and Jonas had stopped by the house and Jonas had ended up arguing with his father. I had asked Jonas if he'd said anything to his father that day about Samuel's helping me with the book. He said he hadn't. But since the day I asked, he hadn't answered my calls. Often in the writing of this book, I got the feeling Jonas was afraid of telling me the exact truth, as if he had a long history of deception behind him and had not yet learned how to come clean.

This was the first time Samuel and I had talked openly about Jonas since the Sunday afternoon I'd told him that Jonas would be part of the book. It had been a cold December day, an unusually cold day in an unusually cold month that gave way to a temperate January. When Samuel saw me in front of the house, he asked me in. Immediately the woodstove heat of the house caught me in its fist. I wanted to stay in the warmth of the woodstove, but I didn't want to delay talking to Samuel any more than I already had. Despite the cold, I asked if he and I could step outside. When we took to his back porch, I told him that I had talked with Jonas and that I was going to include him in the book I was writing. I tried to reassure him that Jonas had nothing bad to say about Amish life.

He was quiet for a minute.

"You are, huh?"

"He seems like a good kid, Samuel. He's not going around trashing the Amish. He just wants to live English."

"Maybe he's too young to know what he wants," Samuel said.

When he said this, Samuel did not seem angry—he seemed wounded.

The conversation soon moved into clichés about young kids with big ideas, about bad apples and good bunches.

"We're too good of friends for this to get in the way," he said.

"I guess I'm asking you to trust me," I said.

"I already trust you. I just don't feel comfortable talking about Jonas."

We left it at that, and telling him had felt good, at least better than not telling him had. Still, it felt like a betrayal.

I still wonder why Samuel has granted me access to his and his people's lives to write this book. I know I've caused him concern and heartache. He has told me several times that he's doing it as a favor to me. "If somebody else asked me, I wouldn't do it." He's also admitted he hopes that "because the book's coming from you, maybe the outside world will realize not all Amish are like they are on TV." And recently Samuel said to me, "We're not really supposed to talk to people about our church, so I wouldn't have done this for anybody else."

Samuel then changed the subject, mentioning that while he was at his nephew's barn raising the other day it was rainy, windy, and sixty-five degrees. He shook his head at the unpredictability of it all.

I stopped by the next day, Monday afternoon, and I found Samuel carrying sacks of feed to the upper story of the barn. I threw a bag over my shoulder and started helping him haul them up.

"You can't be carrying anything this heavy," he said.

The fact that I teach college and write for a living is something Samuel has a hard time understanding. In the Swartzentruber world teaching is woman's work, which is why, I believe, Samuel often jokingly disparages my physical abilities.

When I turned to leave, Samuel said, "See you, Joe," and I felt a sting of guilt, wishing I had never talked to Jonas, knowing I had to.

As I pulled out of the driveway, wondering if Samuel regarded me differently now that I had told him the truth about Jonas—that I was talking to the first of his line to leave the Amish—Samuel's son Jacob squatted behind a burn barrel, playing hide-and-seek with my car. I pulled up, looked over at the burn barrel. He hid. I pulled up again; he poked his head around where I could see it. I backed up. He hid. I pulled up. He poked out his head. We repeated our roles in this undeclared game several times, until when I was least expecting it, Jacob burst from behind the burn barrel and sprinted toward the barn, heading straight for his father.

→ ←

I know I've put Samuel in a tough spot for the last couple of years. If the people of Samuel's church start talking about his helping me, he could be in a dangerous place. Amish scholars call this kind of thing "church trouble," and one even warned me about the worst that could happen. More and more I wonder why Samuel is allowing me access to his people and his story. Does he have a motive he hasn't told me? Samuel is a minister and a deacon. His job, in part, is to visit homes of the wayward and encourage them to confess their wrongs. I didn't realize just how tightly interconnected and wired the community was until a few months later.

Whenever my family is alone with his or whenever Samuel and I spend time together when nobody else is around, it's easy to believe that there is no us and them, that there is nothing separating us, not really. And I believe I have reason to feel this way.

In Samuel's community neighbors help each other. When Samuel and Mary have needed rides to the doctor, Dandi and I have tried to be there for them. Other times we've inserted ourselves squarely in the Amish camp against the English. Several years ago, Samuel's buggy horse broke loose from his reins during an ice storm in Ashland. With the streets nothing but ice, cars could barely move, and neither cars nor horses had any say in where they wound up. The horse ended up running over one car—that's up on the hood, then the roof, then the trunk—before landing on the front end of another car.

Although nobody was hurt—not Samuel, not the driver of either car, not the horse—both cars were totaled. One was brand new and the other looked as though it had seen too many back roads and too many bad accidents. Because of the storm there were numerous accidents in Ashland that day, and Samuel wasn't ticketed. But that still left two totaled cars. The new car had comprehensive insurance, but somebody needed to pay the deductible of $600. Because the Amish do not have insurance on their vehicles, their houses, or any other property, Samuel didn't even know what a deductible was and asked me if the car's owner was on the level. I assured him that because his horse had totaled the guy's car, paying the deductible was his responsibility.

A night or two after the matter of the deductible was settled, the driver of the second car—the owner of the beater that had seen too many roads and too many accidents—showed up at Samuel and Mary's farm. The man, an African American, and his white girlfriend produced a picture of the car they wanted to buy and told the Shetlers how much it cost. They wanted Samuel to pay $5,000 for the car they'd picked out from a dealer.

Writer, farmer, and friend of the Amish Wendell Berry writes that "the [Amish] may well be the last surviving white community of any considerable size in this country." Berry is no doubt right about that characterization. And because of

their all-white communities, where they interact on a daily ba-
sis with people just like themselves, their attitudes about blacks
reveal a dark side of living in such an insular and homogeneous
community. All the Amish ever hear about African Americans
has to do with crime. When I told Samuel that my daughter
was leaving for graduate school in Chicago, he said, "You better
be careful she doesn't come home with a black boyfriend." As it
turns out, the man whose car he totaled did not do much to relieve Samuel of his prejudice. The guy and his girlfriend were
clearly out to take advantage of the ignorant Amish guy who
knew nothing about insurance or how the system worked. I
told Samuel I'd be sure to be at the farm when the couple came
to get the money. In the meantime, I checked out the blue-
book value of the car they'd lost, and it was worth only $1,200.
I told Samuel he owed the couple $1,200, no more, no less. I
brought a copy of the blue-book price with me when the man
and woman showed up. They weren't happy I'd foiled their
plan, but they took the money and left. A couple of days later,
the man showed up again complaining of back pain, and
Samuel gave him a couple hundred dollars more to see a chiropractor.

If the Amish believe the people of the world generally are
not godly, they seem even more wary of worldly African Americans. I've often wondered if this attitude comes solely from being so cut off from diverse groups of people. Maybe they
associate all inner-city crime with blacks. On my less charitable
days, I put some of the blame on the demographic makeup
where I live. Although there are many fine people in Ashland
County, we, like a lot of places in rural America, have our share

of Confederate flags and the attitudes that accompany them. African Americans constitute less than 1 percent of the county's population—and zero percent of the Swartzentruber Amish population. Nobody would accuse Ashland County of being a bastion of liberalism. It's not even a thimble of liberalism.

Just after Samuel and Mary settled the problem with the couple's car and thought the insurance problems were over, they received a letter in the mail stating that they owed State Farm Insurance $18,000, which was the cost of the new car with comprehensive insurance that their horse and the ice storm had destroyed. When State Farm did not get a response, the company sent a registered letter to the Shetlers, threatening to take their farm and their home unless they paid $18,000. Samuel and Mary thought that perhaps the company would take $10 or $20 a month. I started writing letters to State Farm, explaining that the Amish do not purchase insurance because then they would be "yoked" with the outside world, that insurance was at odds with their religious beliefs. I explained to the family that my letters were a long shot, but I didn't tell them just how long a shot I really believed them to be. Samuel and Mary worried, wondering how they'd ever be able to pay this much money. After I wrote several more letters, they received one stating that the company was not going to seek reimbursement. They were delighted. I was stunned.

I naively thought that because I had intervened on their behalf a couple of times, and we had been friends for years, they considered me one of them. But it's not that easy. Whenever a group of Amish, family members or friends, visited Samuel when I was around, I was made to feel my outsider status keenly. Although Samuel would talk to me, it would only be about what he was doing at that moment. When I watched him and some other guys build a neighbor's silo, Samuel would stop work every few minutes and talk to me about how the pulley worked or how tall a silo should be, but there was no discussion of anything more intimate than that, no conversation that said we were anything more than casual acquaintances.

I never felt more the outsider than on a recent May afternoon. I had stopped by the farm as I often do just to say hello. At first I couldn't find Samuel. I hoped he wasn't out in the field, where I'd be faced with the decision to walk all the way out there, or return home having been too lazy to walk out in the field to say hello to a friend. I saw Clara at the produce stand, and in her shy, friendly way, she told me her dad was in the buggy shop. But she never said who was in there with him. I walked in after a light knock on the door, just as I have done numerous times. I sensed immediately that he wished I had not turned up just now. Clearly I had interrupted a serious conversation. Both men stopped talking and turned toward me. A stern silence filled the shop. Samuel was leaning against a work shelf with his arms crossed in front of him. A couple of feet away another Amish man, who looked to be about Samuel's age, posed similarly. Although Samuel turned his head in my direction and said a polite hello, his body language suggested that I was clearly there as an outsider. An unwanted and unwelcome presence. He did not turn toward me or initiate any small talk. His allegiance was clear and so was his message. He wanted me gone. I've experienced this with Samuel before. He has the ability both to make me feel like his finest friend—or finest English friend—on earth, and to make me feel my outsider status in a stinging way. Samuel had no intention of introducing me or in saying another word while I was there. I walked out of the buggy shop.

I didn't stop by to visit for a couple of weeks after this, and when I did the first thing Samuel did is invite me inside his home to get out of the rain, which had been falling unendingly for the past five days. The house was filled with the heat from the cookstove because Mary had butter bubbling in a large cast-iron frying pan.

"You know the day you came over when I was in the buggy shop?" Samuel asked. "That was my bishop."

"Something intense seemed to be going on." I waited for Samuel to respond to my not-so-subtle query about the content of their conversation.

"I just didn't want you to mention anything about the book," he said.

I told him that of course I'd never mention the book to an Amish person I didn't know, and Samuel said that he knew I wouldn't.

But I was reminded of what Samuel has to lose in a situation like this. He is an honorable man who is loyal to his Amish life, his Ordnung, his church, and his family. He is also a minister, one of only two in his church district. And he is still a deacon because they have not been able to find another deacon to take his place now that he's a minister. As a deacon, one of Samuel's duties is to confront members of the church who have violated or disobeyed the church rules. If a member uses a chainsaw, he'll find the deacon at his door. A deacon might even show up if a member is giving an English person private information about the workings of Swartzentruber Amish life. If Samuel's bishop learned of his cooperation with his book and told him to stop immediately, Samuel would have to do that or be in church trouble. He could even be excommunicated and shunned. However, it's much more likely he'd just stop talking to me. The bishop's word is final and his authority unquestioned, and yet here is Samuel, who has let me into his life in a way few English have ever been invited into the daily lives of the Swartzentruber Amish.

To make matters worse, Samuel's bishop is also Jonas's uncle.

→ ←

Jonas's suspicions about me all these months later are not merely a product of paranoia. The Amish do keep an eye on each other. What outsiders see as getting into somebody else's business or ratting out a friend, the Amish I know consider a dire responsibility to keep members in the church. Jonas experienced this firsthand when he tried to leave and his neighbor Levi interfered. And the church has been pressuring Jonas's father more and more, telling him that he's not doing enough to encourage Jonas to come home. Lately, Menno has begun to work with the church against his son.

One day in particular seemed to be a seminal day in Jonas's relationship with his dad and his church. Menno had agreed to meet Jonas at the local sawmill where Jonas had once worked. Although Menno is a carpenter for Amish and English alike, for the last six months he's been working at the sawmill, almost as if he's taken Jonas's place, as if he's been forced to take Jonas's place, which would not be uncommon among these Swartzentruber Amish. Samuel has told me that the church has been having some problems with its carpenters.

Too many Amish carpenters have been making too much money working on English homes. Because the money is so good, usually over fifteen dollars an hour, the carpenters have been working twelve- and fourteen-hour days, which means that they are away from home for that long or longer, depending on the commute. The Swartzentruber Amish have done a good job of keeping most of their people on the farm, which means that father, mother, and children are home together almost all day every day—the way it should be. Unlike some more modern Amish who are permitted to be picked up by a van driven by an English guy in order to work on construction crews, the Swartzentrubers are not. They have to drive their buggies wherever the job is. One carpenter has had six buggy accidents in the last couple of years. "If he hadn't been gone so often, he wouldn't have had that many accidents," Samuel said. "If he stayed home and had a shop, he could make as much money as he could make." Samuel's church decided that something had to be done. The ordained men of the church group gathered and decided that no carpenter could charge the English over ten dollars an hour. Again, the community trumps the individual. What one Amish person does affects other Amish.

These same carpenters are also expected to work on Amish jobs at a much reduced rate. For example, Samuel was charged twenty dollars per eight-hour day, per carpenter, for work done on his new house. This is the power of the church in an individual's life. The fact that Menno now worked at the sawmill instead of as a carpenter could be seen as evidence that he had been cooperating with the church, by taking over his son's job. Jonas believes it has more to do with the church clamping down on a carpenter's wages, making working at the sawmill more attractive.

It was at the mill that Menno had agreed to meet with Jonas. Jonas had hoped his father would bring a copy of his marriage license, so that Jonas could obtain his passport and a Social Security number. At the very least he needed the marriage certificate, which he could get a copy of through Canadian records only if his parents were deceased. Jonas had high hopes when Menno agreed to meet him at the sawmill at noon on a Saturday. Although Jonas wished for the best and could not help feeling hopeful, he kept telling himself it wasn't going to happen, just so he wouldn't be disappointed. There was no way his dad was simply going to hand over his marriage license. When his dad showed up at noon on that day, he told Jonas he would not give him the certificate, nor would he sign an affidavit stating how long he had lived in the country. Jonas understood then that the church had gotten to his father. And he was right. Menno told Jonas there was nothing he could do for him.

"That's what upsets me about the Amish," Jonas says. "I wish my dad wouldn't have to go through all that. The church is so two-faced."

From that day on Menno has refused to see his son. A few weeks ago, Nora and Jonas were driving to town in her truck when they hit a deer. The deer wound up in a ditch and the truck's front end was banged up pretty good. When Jonas and Nora were on the side of the road with the dented truck and the dead doe, the English woman who lives across the street from Jonas's parents drove by. Now, Jonas thought, she'll tell my dad I was in an accident and he'll come to see me. For four or five days, anytime a buggy rolled up or down Nora's street, day or night, Jonas ran to the window. And every day he was disappointed. "I guess my dad's not coming," Jonas finally said.

Although not officially excommunicated and shunned because he has not been baptized, Jonas is definitely getting the unofficial version of the stiff arm that is shunning.

The idea of being separate—and of separating others—runs throughout Amish life. The Amish see themselves as separate from the world and they separate themselves from the world in accordance with Romans 12:2 and 2 Corinthians 6:14. The former says, "Be not conformed to this world, but be ye transformed by the renewing of your mind that ye may prove what is that good and acceptable and perfect will of God." And the latter: "Be ye not equally yoked together with unbelievers; for what fellowship hath righteousness with unrighteousness? What communion hath light with darkness?"

Imposed separateness occurs when a person is excommunicated.

When any one, after he is enlightened, has accepted the knowledge of the truth, and been incorporated into the communion of saints, sins again unto death, either through willfulness, or through presumption against God . . . thereby becoming separated from God . . . such a one, after the deed is manifest and sufficiently known to the church, may not remain in the congregation of the righteous . . . and must be separated. (Dordrecht Confession of Faith, Article XVI)

An Amish person can be excommunicated for a few weeks or forever. A person who voluntarily or involuntarily leaves the fold after baptism is excommunicated and shunned. Shunning somebody who has been excommunicated strengthens the community, reinforcing to everybody the idea that the weakest link has been removed, and that the chain of community has been made even stronger. According to Kraybill, "Shunning does not reflect personal animosity, but rather it is a ritual means of shaming the wayward . . . Conversation is not forbidden, but members may not shake hands or accept anything directly from the offender." And yet, with a willingness to obey the rules, a public confession, and a probationary period, even somebody who has been excommunicated and shunned for fifty years could, theoretically, return to the church. Nothing about Amish life seems more repellant to the English than shunning. How could a parent shun a son or daughter? A wife her husband? A child his mother? What's with these strange people? But according to one Amish man in the know, "Shunning is their last way of showing you that they love you."

Now Jonas is in a no-man's-land, cut off from his family in an unofficial shunning, and not yet English. He's also a man without a country. Although born in Canada, he feels no allegiance to the country. Although an American citizen, he has nothing to prove it. Jonas does not want to end up merely ex-

Amish. It's clear there are Amish, ex-Amish, and English. The ex-Amish hold on to many Amish ways, trying to incorporate them into the English world. Jonas's friend Noah is an example. Although he's been out for several years, he still does not have a strong footing in the English world. He has yet to earn his GED, or to even start the process. His speech is heavily Amish-accented English, and he's still partying every chance he gets. He'll often hang around with other ex-Amish and speak Amish while he parties. The cousin of Jonas's father, on the other hand, who's been out for eight years, speaks nearly unaccented English. Nobody who did not know the Amish would ever be able to tell he had once been a member of the ultra-conservative Swartzentruber Amish.

Jonas hopes his life will mirror his cousin's, but he's beginning to lose hope. Nothing seems to be working out the way he thought it would, and now he knows that his father has chosen the church over his son.

NINE

Time and Space

On a July morning that promises a day of ninety degrees and suffocating humidity, I'm boarding Samuel's buggy. I'm delighted we'll have two horses pulling the buggy today, which should mean an easier trip for all concerned. Two horsepower is better than one. Samuel and Mary sold their old driver to an English guy six months ago, and he's been replaced by Honey, who takes her place alongside Heather, who's been around for a few years. I can't help noticing that since I've been hanging out with Samuel more than usual for the last couple of years, I regard the weather as singularly important. I find myself wondering about it more and more, asking my wife if she's heard a forecast, watching the sky, the trees, and the animals, even if I'll be inside writing for the entire day. Weather is everything to a farmer, especially an Amish farmer. Although Samuel does not want to leave as early as we're leaving, the impending heat and humidity make leaving at dawn imperative. Making the trip in the afternoon would be much harder on the horses, which could mean they'd need more time to rest and might not be available if there's another buggy trip needed later that day. We're going to Home Depot so Samuel can pick up some supplies for the new house he's building. It will take us an hour and a half to go ten miles, three hours round trip, plus the time in the store. If we're lucky, we'll be back by noon.

The new house is a bit of a compromise dream. Although Samuel dreams often of moving out west, he knows that's not likely to happen, not as long as Mary's family is around. So a new house, extending twelve feet farther west than the original house, will be as far west as Samuel's bound to get. When Samuel and Mary moved into the original house, they had three kids, which made living arrangements pretty comfortable. Now they have nine kids, including several teenagers. Even Amish teenagers like their privacy. Mary's always wanted a big bedroom and a pantry that people moving between her house and the dawdy haus don't have to pass through. She also wants more closets. And now that the house is almost finished, the whole family is starting to make plans for it. The girls have picked out their new rooms. Now each girl will have to share a bed with only one sister. The boys are ecstatic—they'll finally have a bedroom of their own.

On this day, Samuel has a boy over helping out. Peter is from a family in Samuel's district. Because Samuel and Mary have been so busy with the house, it's been up to the kids to do most of the chores. A hired boy can pick up a lot of the slack. Peter, having just finished the eighth grade in May, started working the first of the month and will most likely be here for the entire month, maybe more, during which he'll work alongside the family doing anything Samuel needs him to do, as well as eating meals with them, praying with them, and sleeping in their house. All the money fourteen-year-old Peter makes from working at Samuel's place will go to his parents. When he turns twenty-one, the money he makes will be his to keep.

Peter hitches up the horses and brings the buggy to the road. Samuel hops in effortlessly. I lift my leg to the pedal-sized runner called a buggy step and pull myself up into the buggy seat, trying to look natural and agile or, at the very least, not foolish. Samuel says something to Peter in Pennsylvania Dutch, and the boy disappears into the house. He returns with two cups of coffee prepared by Mary. "See these cups a seed salesman gave me?" Samuel asks. "Do you know what they're made out of?" Whenever Samuel asks me a question like this, I know better than to venture an answer, so I tell him I have no idea. "Corn," he says. As I squeeze the cup and acknowledge that it feels more like a hard rubber than plastic, I'm grateful I didn't attempt to guess. Samuel loves this kind of discovery. And he loves that I don't know all I don't know. In the field the other day he pointed to what looked to me like giant leaves and vines sprouting from the ground. "Do you know what those are?" he asked. I said no as quickly as I could, but this wasn't enough for him. He waited a few seconds. "You'll know what they are around Halloween." Pumpkins, I get it. When we're situated with our coffee, Samuel covers his legs with a heavy dark-blue blanket and tells me I'd better take my half of the blanket because it's cold first thing in the morning in a buggy. I do what he says.

Cars speed by us as we roll along at five miles per hour when the horses are walking, ten to twelve when they begin a trot. The steel wheels roll noisily along the pocked, paved road. The rush and power of the cars flying by frightens me and, quite frankly, pisses me off. Although I have done it thousands of times myself, I'm angry that people out here pass buggies like they're not even there, ignoring the danger and frightening the horses. I'm grateful it's early morning; at least it's not dark. Every thinking English driver around here is on high alert at night, because there are no reflecting orange-and-red slow-moving vehicle signs and no battery-powered lights on Swartzen-truber buggies. It's dangerous to come upon them in the dark, when you're traveling at fifty and they're traveling at ten, because it's difficult to see them while you still have enough time to brake and pass. In nearby counties with "higher church," or more liberal Old Order groups, driving at night is far safer and easier on the nerves. Some buggies even have orange battery-powered lights on the back that spin inside a plastic globe like lights on a cop car. But the Swartzentrubers reject the lights, so buggies on the road at night will be a dangerous presence as long as there are Swartzentruber Amish.

The buggy defines Amish life. It's iconic and symbolic; practical and dangerous. Every cheesy calendar or coffee-table book claiming to depict Amish life will feature buggies: buggies at dusk and dawn, buggies with autumn leaves in the background, buggies rolling along beneath fat flakes of falling snow. The Amish—except for the Beachy Amish—reject the car absolutely. As Donald B. Kraybill writes, "[Buggies] link members together in common history and a common mission against worldliness . . . they draw the boundary lines between church and world. As badges of ethnicity, they announce Amish identity to insider and outsider alike. In many ways they are sacred symbols, which the Amish have guarded with care." Although most orders will hire a van or at least somebody to drive them places, the Swartzentrubers will accept rides from English friends only when the trip involves a doctor visit or in some other rare instance, like the time I drove Samuel to Canada for his mother's funeral. The same reason I and most other Americans love our cars is the reason the Amish reject them: ease of mobility. The Amish have not thrived in this country by making it easy for their people to take off on a whim.

Although this is not my first ride in a buggy it will be my longest. My first buggy ride with Samuel was to a produce auction just a few miles away. I arrived at Samuel's at our agreed-upon time, understanding immediately that Samuel would not be ready to leave for the auction for quite some time. There was still work to be done. Samuel had invited me along several times, but this was the first time I'd been able to say yes. He and Mary stood on the stoop of the produce stand cleaning and separating red peppers into good ones and cutters; cutters are seconds cut up for cooking. There were also hot, long green peppers. A wheelbarrow full of damaged red peppers sat nearby, and it had "pig food" written all over it.

"It will be like music playing to the pigs when they get these peppers," Samuel said. (This coming from a man who's forbidden to listen to music.)

Flies surrounded the produce stand as if they'd waited their entire tiny lives for a feast of this magnitude.

Baby David cried a bit from inside the house, sounding like he might be hungry. Everybody was working, Barbara cleaning up gourds, Andy wiping down the hot peppers and placing them in baskets, Jacob and Clara bringing the buggy up to the front of the stand to be loaded. Clara stood in place of a horse, rickshaw style, while Jacob pushed a wheel from behind. Seeing them struggle to move the buggy up the slight incline, Grandpa

Shetler hurried over to help. Even two-year-old Esther played at helping by washing a pepper or two and placing them somewhere her parents didn't want them to go. Samuel ran to the barn and brought back his younger buggy horse, Heather, who at the time was a two-year-old without too much road time alone, without the age and experience of Samuel's other drivers.

After we'd loaded the buggy, we had some trouble getting Heather to pull us out of the driveway and onto the road. Samuel got out of the buggy, grabbed the horse's harness, and pulled Heather out on the road. His dad came out and said, in German, that there was too much weight in the buggy. I knew he wasn't talking about the weight of the produce. He wasn't even speaking strictly of my physical weight. By the "weight" of the English, he'd meant, at least in part, the constant tension and friction that acts like an invisible electric fence between the Swartzentruber Amish world and the modern world, the English world, my world. Although the Swartzentrubers—like most Amish—are taught to limit their interactions with the English to matters of business and simple civility, sometimes personalities eclipse practice. The Swartzentrubers have not maintained their extreme and legendary traditionalism by letting English loiter in their midst. While Mr. Shetler is always civil, courteous, quick with a hello or a story, and grateful that I drove his son to his wife's funeral all those years ago, he is far more careful in his dealings with me. I have not been invited into his house for dinner or homemade ice cream, although he has given me a fistful of raspberries from bushes near the entrance of his buggy shop. I have never been invited to ride along in his buggy. Whenever I'm around him I get the feeling that he is part of a tightly woven fabric, and that he's afraid my being around too much will cause there to be a loose thread, hardly visible, that could, if not repaired, loosen the fabric until it has the consistency of mesh.

When we got Heather going and headed east on 620, Samuel told me our rough start had nothing to do with any extra weight, but had to do instead with the laziness of Heather.

On the way to the auction Samuel did most of the talking. He talked about how he liked Heather's gait and how one day she'd make a fine buggy horse. The Amish folks we passed threw Samuel grins. He hollered out to a few of them, calling me his helper, and a laugh was shared at my expense.

When we got to the auction I helped Samuel unload, and then I entered into the mystery of a country produce auction. The auction was basically split evenly between Amish and English. Pickup trucks and horse-drawn wagons carried loads of corn, squash, cantaloupe, gourds, and assorted other fruits and vegetables, taking their places with each other in the same lines. Gazing out over a wagon filled with sun-topped pumpkins at dusk, I saw nothing but buggies and horses and produce. I could have been gazing into the nineteenth century.

Because I didn't bring any money with me, I borrowed a dollar from Samuel for a bottle of water.

"If you're hungry take my wallet and get something to eat," Samuel said.

"No thanks."

"I'm getting a little hungry myself."

At the auction I saw the son of the Amish man from whom I buy my firewood. He told me I was the best firewood buyer they had, which filled me, inexplicably, with pride. I've bought at least five loads each of the last few years, and a year ago I bested even myself and bought eight pickup-truck loads. The boy has molasses-black hair that sticks out in curls from under his hat. He also has a wide and easy smile revealing bright, white teeth.

An Amish man pulling a cartload of collapsed cardboard boxes had some trouble getting through a doorway, so an English woman dressed in denim helped him through the doorway by moving one of the boxes out of the way, in effect tucking it in.

The auction was endless. The gibberish that passed for auctioneering was equally endless. I prayed for it to end.

When Samuel decided he'd had enough, we made our way out to the buggy with our own stash of collapsed cardboard boxes, which Samuel would use for the next auction. There had to have been fifty identical buggies tied to a rail, but Samuel walked right to his, where Heather stood waiting for us, nickering to other members of her species.

As we were about to back out, Samuel noticed that one of the horses tied up next to his had nudged free of his bridle.

"I don't like the look of that," he said. "That's too new-looking of a buggy to have these horses taking off."

Samuel placed the bridle back on the horse, secured the reins to the hitching post, and we were off. He offered me one of Mary's sandwiches, made with her homemade bread, marble cheese, and garden tomatoes. I readily accepted.

"This sandwich puts me in mind of that guy in Buffalo who I made the sandwich for. He had tears in his eyes, he was so grateful."

Samuel proceeded to tell me a story about a guy he met on a bus going from Cleveland to Toronto. The man claimed to be a homeless veteran. At first Samuel didn't believe him because he didn't believe a vet could be homeless. He was under the mistaken impression that America cared for each and every one of its veterans. The man asked Samuel a lot of questions about the Amish. Samuel said he didn't like the scene because he didn't know the guy's agenda. When the bus stopped in Erie, Pennsylvania, the guy asked Samuel if he'd lend him money for a can of pop because he only had a quarter and a penny. He gave Samuel the quarter and Samuel bought him a pop, leaving the guy with a penny. When the bus stopped in Buffalo, the homeless veteran asked Samuel if he'd lend him money to have lunch at a restaurant outside the bus station. Instead, Samuel made him a tomato sandwich with mayonnaise and cheese.

The horses clip-clopped through the quintessential country night—cool breeze, the sun just going down, perfectly round and red.

"The best time of the day," Samuel said.

When he offered me a pear, I accepted, and we rode in silence as we ate, a black blanket pulled up over our knees, hearing nothing but the country music of horse hooves and the grinding roll of the buggy wheels on the road.

→ ←

But one ride is not nearly enough to get a pampered English man comfortable with the bareness of a Swartzentruber Amish buggy. While the more liberal Old Order Amish buggies have windshields, rearview mirrors, hydraulic brakes, bright upholstery, the slow-moving vehicle sign, a small rear window, a high dashboard, and twelve-volt lights, the Swartzentruber buggies have not one of these accessories. Even the Andy Weaver Amish, a subaffiliation of the Old Order who are less traditional than the Swartzentrubers but more traditional than the Old Order, are permitted the slow-moving vehicle sign, rear window, high dashboards, and twelve-volt lights. The New Order Amish have everything the Old Order have plus rubber tires, sliding doors, wipers, and plush upholstery. As is the case with all things, the Swartzentrubers are Spartan about their buggies. The normal single-seat buggy is five feet long and twenty-six inches wide (two-seaters are eight feet long and thirty-four inches wide), with wheels that are thirty-eight inches on the front and forty-two on the back. The wheels are made of wood with a band of steel wrapped around to meet the road. Springs in the front and back act as shocks to ease the ride of steel and wood on bumpy country roads. The top of the buggy is covered with black oil-cloth that snaps onto the wood. A new single-seat carriage will cost about $1,400 in these parts. I sit on what we American car owners consider the driver's side, and Samuel operates the buggy from the passenger's side, the right side, which is customary in Swartzentruber buggies. A twenty-six-inch-long brake handle rises up just a couple of inches higher than the seat, making it easy for the driver to push the section of steel covered with rubber against the steel of the wheel, in much the same way that drivers did in stagecoaches and carriages more than a century ago. The driver pulls the brake handle so it pushes against the right front wheel, then pulls on the reins. If all is going well, the horses and buggy will stop.

But all does not always go well.

Just three weeks before the day Samuel and I rode to Home Depot, an Amish man in a buggy was killed by a car. Less than three weeks after that, two of Samuel's nieces, ages fifteen and nineteen, were pulling out onto the road after the Wednesday-night produce auction when a van they didn't see struck their horse. The woman driving the van said she'd steered toward the horse to avoid hitting the buggy. Hitting the buggy at forty-five miles an hour could have killed the two girls. The horse had to be put down. Two of Samuel and Mary's daughters, Barbara, age fourteen, and Clara, twelve, had taken the family buggy to the same auction. One of the worst buggy accidents Samuel has ever heard of involved a couple he and Mary knew. The husband and wife had just moved out of their house and were heading over to bring a few things to their new home, including a large metal drum, no doubt filled with something heavy. As they rode through the downtown of a small village, the horses spooked and took off. The man could not regain control of the horses before they hit a fire hydrant, which stopped them cold. The man was dumped out of the buggy and onto the street. The woman was also thrown from her seat. She slammed into a telephone pole and was killed when the heavy metal drum flew out of the buggy and smashed her against the pole. The man lived, and a few years later he married the widow of a man who had drowned while swimming in a pond.

→ ←

As we ride, Honey and Heather appear to take turns raising their tails and defecating not two feet from our faces. Honey and Heather are related; they are half-siblings—same mother, different father. Samuel considers their mother, Bell, an all-purpose horse. Even though she's a bit heavy for a road horse, she can be used to pull a buggy; and even though she's a bit small for the field work, she can hold her own among four or five plow horses pulling a thresher or a binder. The good country people of Ashland County have tried to force the Amish to have their horses wear sacklike diapers to catch dropping manure. They've even suggested making a law requiring the Amish to pick up the mess made by their horses, which set off a stream of letters to the editor in the local paper. Over 80 percent of the letter writers wanted something done about the manure. My wife and I wrote a letter, simply asking how harmful horse droppings were as compared to car exhaust. We decided we'd take horse manure over carbon monoxide any day. Horses and buggies are the source of aggravation and venom from a lot of people in Amish country. The only thing they hate more than manure on the road is a horse and buggy on the road. For years the Amish have cut down trees and done favors for people living in a gated community in Ashland County. Ostensibly because of the manure—although talking to people I got the feeling that some did not want the Amish in their gated utopia at all—the community elders tried to say the bylaws forbid horses, which would, in effect, forbid Amish. After some folks complained and others scoured the community's bylaws and weren't able to find any ordinance barring horses from entering, the topic was dropped. And then talk turned to the possibility of E. coli. Fear got hold of me and I started wondering if those diaper sacks were really all that bad. Soon the letter writing and outcries waned, and then stopped, but the controversy will not go away. Nor will other controversies concerning the Amish around here.

It's been my experience that people who live in this community surrounded by the Amish either love them or hate them—there does not appear to be much middle ground. The haters see nothing good about them. All they do see is a people they're convinced are getting away with something. They don't like the manure and they don't like the dirt or the bare feet. When I was in West Salem's only grocery store one day, I was in line behind a Swartzentruber Amish woman. After she had paid for her food and was walking out, the cashier waved her hand in front of her nose, as if warding off an unpleasant odor. Although there's no doubt that working hard every day and bathing only on Saturday evenings can make somebody a bit ripe, I was offended by the gesture and told the cashier what I thought. She told me that if I worked there and had to put up with it all the time, I'd complain too. I didn't want to start an argument, so I let it go. Only later did it strike me that the cashier herself—an African American woman in a nearly all-white community—might have been the subject of such rudeness in the not too distant past.

A lot of the Amish bashers seem particularly perturbed that Amish children don't go to school beyond the eighth grade. Someone told me recently that she thinks the government ought to step in and force the Amish to give their kids a better education. This same person had no idea that the Supreme Court ruled in favor of the Amish not having to send their children to public high schools in *Wisconsin v. Yoder* in 1972. Chief Justice Warren Berger's opinion read, in part, "almost 300 years of consistent practice, and strong evidence of sustained faith pervading and regulating respondents' entire mode of life support the claim that enforcement of the State's requirement of compulsory formal education after the eighth grade would gravely endanger if not destroy the free exercise of respondents' religious beliefs."

More than anything else, I believe some modern folks loathe the Amish because they're a flesh-and-blood symbol of all America has rejected and all the Amish reject of America. The Amish are perceived as being anti-progress, as refuting the economy we've created, and a society we've accepted. I believe those who loathe the Amish feel guilty because the Amish take care of their elderly and sick without the help of the state or the cost of insurance. They don't like the fact that the Amish have far fewer expenses than the rest of us do and that they've bought up so much land over the years. They're bothered by the fact that the Amish have no car or house payments to make, no insurance premiums, no jobs they hate, no retirement they're aching for, no nursing homes, no extravagant health-care costs.

They especially don't want the Amish to get any special treatment, particularly if their taxes have to pay for it. Buggy lanes, for example. In some areas heavily populated with buggies, municipalities have considered adding buggy lanes to the roads, which would be for buggies only and would not cut into car lanes. Because this always involves money, of course, not to mention numerous residents selling or giving up sections of their land that meet the road, the issue has come up and gone away several times. An Ohio representative proposed a bill in 2001 that would have helped the twenty-one counties that are home to the state's Amish. The bill was designed to help pay for wider berms and for educating English about driving safely in Amish country. September 11 of that year eclipsed the bill. Although there was only one fatal buggy accident in 2005—there have already been two in 2006—there were still 148 buggy accidents that year. In 2001, when the bill was proposed, buggies were involved in 129 accidents. Buggy-on-buggy accidents are unheard of, and if they happen, they're not reported.

Some deriders of the Amish are under the impression that the Amish do not pay taxes, which is not true. They pay real estate, federal, state, and local taxes and refuse government farm subsidies. This does not mean that every single Amish person pays income taxes, in the same way not every non-Amish person pays taxes. But the Amish are required by law to pay taxes, and the Amish I know do not seek out trouble; they figure enough of it will come their way without their going to look for it. The Amish do not pay into Social Security, nor do they accept any Social Security benefits. (An Amish man who hires English workers does have to pay into Social Security for them.) A number of Amish bishops petitioned the government, citing a Bible passage that reads as follows: "But if any provide not for his own, and specially for those of his own house, he hath denied the faith, and is worse than an infidel" (1 Tim. 5:8). After all, it's the job of the community to care for its elderly. The Amish also eschew any kind of insurance, be it home or life. As Kraybill writes, "insurance programs—especially life insurance plans—are viewed as gambling ventures that seek to plan and protect one's fortunes rather than yield them to the will of God."

Samuel has told me numerous times that he has all the insurance he needs and it is his church. When a tornado touched down on a neighboring farm in November of 2004, an Amish barn was destroyed. Within a week, a new barn was rebuilt by a crew made up of just about every able-bodied Amish man in the vicinity. The owner of the barn was expected to buy the material, if possible; otherwise a collection would be made. I have witnessed the community in action many times over the years. The community takes care of everybody within it from the cradle to the grave. My wife and I have chastised ourselves for not being involved enough in our community of neighbors, friends, and colleagues. The Amish have taught us something about what it means to watch out for each other. When we had a family of skunks living under our shed, Samuel came over unannounced on a ninety-degree day after a long afternoon spent working on his chicken coop. He parked his two plow horses and his wagon in our driveway. He dug up dirt to use as a barrier, so the skunks wouldn't be able to escape once the smoke bombs went off. By the time he left to do his evening chores, his shirt was drenched and he had helped a helpless English friend. Their dedication to community often stretches well beyond their own.

→ ←

As we drive, I look around and imagine what I would do if I had to jump clear of the buggy—if, for instance, the horses got frightened and were headed for a ditch that would surely tip us, or a semi truck lost control and came barreling at us. How could I jump free of steel wheels and horse hooves? I see no easy way. Luckily, Samuel is as competent a driver as he is everything else and we arrive at Home Depot without incident. Because there are no hitching posts, Samuel ties the horses to a lamppost a good distance from the store.

I soon learn that—if Samuel and I are any example—Amish men, unlike people who drive, don't speed to a store, dart in, get what they need, and get out. The horses need a rest before the drive back, and Samuel is going to take his time picking out what he needs. Now that his new house is ready for drywall, he has to buy some more insulation, some molding, paint, and primer. After we've walked around together for about twenty minutes, I leave Samuel's side to find something to fix a broken lamp at home. Samuel shops for material the way my mother-in-law hunts for off-season bargains. His goal is to get what he needs at the lowest possible price, no matter how much he has to look or how much time it takes. Although that may be the goal of many English shoppers too, I have been known to grab whatever I need, proceed to the register, and throw plastic at the price. The Swartzentruber Amish, of course, do not use credit or credit cards. Samuel knows exactly what he has to spend. If he runs out of money, the house will be short the paint or molding or whatever until he has the money. Because of this, the man takes his time, figuring everything out to the penny.

When I leave him to his calculations, I decide to see just how many things Home Depot carries that Samuel will never have to buy. All electric appliances are out, of course. I imagine lamps disappearing from the store, and with them all electricity-related paraphernalia: lightbulbs, sockets, cords, adapters . . . Because all big-ticket items run on electricity, the

Swartzentrubers do not need to look at refrigerators, stoves (unless there's a woodburner around), freezers, or air-conditioning units. All the fancy front doors are unnecessary. There's no need for the aisles of tile, linoleum, or carpet. He could buy hammer and nails if he needed them, as well as wrenches and manual screwdrivers. The hardware aisle seems pretty solid for Swartzentruber shoppers. The only paint colors Samuel would ever buy would be white, gray, or some shade of dark blue.

If Samuel were not a Swartzentruber but were instead a member of the Andy Weaver Amish, he'd be able to have linoleum or varnished floors, couches and cushioned chairs, and an indoor toilet, tub, and shower. But no. If he and his family were members of the Old Order, he could have everything permitted by the Andy Weaver Amish plus window blinds, continuous hot water, and central heating. But no. And if he were to join an even higher church than the Old Order and become New Order, he'd have everything in this paragraph plus bottled gas appliances, a gas freezer, and natural gas lighting, which would mean no more kerosene lanterns. But no. All four of these groups do share something, however. Everybody is allowed to have a washing machine—although a washing machine needs to be stripped of anything electrical and must have a belt that runs to a small gasoline engine. And nobody's allowed to have carpeting. I like to imagine all the women of the four orders somehow putting pressure on their husbands, explaining how difficult it would be to do the wash by hand for the two of them plus eight or ten or twelve kids, insisting on making washing machines cool with the Ordnung, or else. Maybe they conceded carpeting as a compromise.

But that's not all. Some New Order affiliations use computers and electric typewriters, and the most liberal New Orders can fly in planes, use a garden tiller, and have a private telephone. Along with the New Order, the Old Order Amish can artificially inseminate (animals not people), use power lawnmowers and weed eaters, hire vehicles, and ride bikes. Even the Andy Weaver Amish can hire a car and driver and own power chainsaws, but not so the Swartzentrubers.

Swartzentruber farmers have lots of room to complain. The New Order Amish can use everything on their farms, including haybines, hay crimpers, corn pickers, mechanical gutter cleaners, and milking machines. The Old and New Order Amish can use portable feed mixers, forklifts, and front-end loaders. Even the Andy Weavers are permitted an elevator in their barns. Although none of the four can use tractors for plowing, the New Order Amish can use them as road vehicles, and even the Andy Weavers and the Old Orders can use tractors around the barn.

But no, not the Swartzentrubers.

Although it often does not appear so to outside observers, there's good reason for the Swartzentrubers' steadfast refusal to make things easy on themselves. As Donald Kraybill writes, "The Swartzentrubers . . . have created a tighter and more restrictive social world [than the more liberal Amish]—one sharply separated from the larger society, which makes it much more difficult to defect. Those who want to abandon their church must jump across a much wider cultural gulf than those in the Old Order or New Order groups. The Swartzentrubers' conservative use of technology surely reflects a more restrictive and rigid consciousness that is shaped by a high degree of social regimentation."

Samuel gets a kick out of it when the cashier at Home Depot says she can help him and then turns to tell me I'll be next. "We're together," Samuel says, smiling.

After we load the buggy with insulation, furring strips, paint, and several five-gallon buckets of primer that we can fit only by putting them up front and sticking our legs out the sides of the buggy, we head home.

I hear a horn and am suddenly in a panic. But then I notice it's my daughter driving into town. She blows the horn again when she passes us on the way back.

The sudden fear caused by a car horn stays with me for the rest of the buggy ride.

TEN

Deadly Sacred

Today was one of those days. I've had them every so often over the last sixteen years I've lived among the Swartzentruber Amish. They're the kind of day I never discuss with Samuel or Mary. I wouldn't dare. Generally I don't say the words out loud, but I will write them: What the hell are you doing living the way you're living? The source of my angst today is word of another buggy accident. That's two buggy fatalities in the last month, both just a few miles from the Shetler farm.

When I was over visiting the other day, I stopped in the buggy shop to see Mr. Shetler. At seventy-five he still works in his buggy shop six days a week, twelve hours a day, and has enough work to last him the rest of his life. I noticed he was selling old buggy wheels for twenty-five dollars apiece. Thinking one might look cool in front of my house, I told him I'd be back with my truck to pick one up. When I arrived that Wednesday morning, the wheel was waiting for me, but then I saw two other wheels prepped for a new buggy, painted all black. I decided that I wanted a black one too. Mr. Shetler said he'd paint it black for an extra two dollars. When I told him I'd pick it up the next day, he told me to make it late in the afternoon because they had a funeral to attend.

"Oh, that's too bad. I'm sorry. Who's it for?" I asked.

"Another buggy accident. Didn't you hear? Some old lady, eighty-nine years old."

"Seventy-nine," his wife yelled from the front porch of the dawdy haus.

It took a while before I understood that a seventy-nine-year-old English woman driving a minivan had smashed into the back of a buggy the previous Sunday afternoon.

"It was daylight. She must not have been paying attention," Mr. Shetler said. "She cried, but it was all done by then."

The woman had been driving southbound on State Route 42, just a few miles from where Samuel and I had been riding on our way to Home Depot not that long ago. The weather was clear; the sun was out, roads dry. Having been out visiting, a Sunday-afternoon Amish pastime, the family was heading home when the accident happened. At five thirty Sunday afternoon the woman plowed her van into the rear end of the buggy. All the buggy's passengers were ejected. All but the father and the baby were taken by ambulance to the local hospital and then life-flighted to Cleveland.

An eight-year-old girl was killed. Her name was Elizabeth. Elizabeth had been riding with her mother, father, two sisters, and two brothers, including the five-month-old baby boy. The father was not injured; nor was the baby. Elizabeth's mother fractured a bone in her neck but would be all right; one of the boys broke a leg and one of the girls suffered a broken collarbone. A picture in the local paper told much of the story: the buggy lay in splinters on the road. The horse was fine.

"Is Samuel around?" I asked, apropos of nothing.

"He's over Levi's thrashing speltz."

Amish girls always get the worst of it. This is what I was thinking after I said good-bye to Mr. Shetler, telling him I'd come by the next day to pick up my wheel, a wheel I no longer wanted. I've loved my rides in Samuel's buggy and I particularly loved telling people about them, as if I were playing a small part in some quaint drama most people could only watch.

But the reality of the life can be as cold, harsh, and cruel as a crash. A splintered buggy. A family spilled out onto the road. A dead eight-year-old girl.

Why not just have a car? Don't you know how dangerous those cute carriages are? Do you really believe wood can hold its own against two tons of steel and whatever the hell else cars are made out of these days? Is it really that important to have a buggy? Can't you just dress oddly but drive cars? Hell, the Mennonites do it. Even the Beachy Amish do it. Don't you know English people drive like lunatics? Why do the Swartzentrubers have to always be the plainest of the plain people? Do you think God cares that the bands around your hats are five-eighths of an inch wide or that you bathe only once a week? Does God really care how wide your hat brims are or whether a woman wears a black or white cap? Does God care that you drive a buggy and I drive a car? Is sticking with your sacred buggies more important than the sanctity of human life? Can't you take care of your children?

This last question buckles my knees in shame.

I already know what Samuel will say when I talk to him about the accident. He'll first give me all the details, which he will have learned from the Swartzentruber grapevine. He'll end up knowing far more than the papers will write or the county's residents will read. (As a matter of fact, with the accident happening on a Sunday, Monday's paper had news of the event; Tuesday's paper announced the death of Elizabeth. Wednesday's paper had nothing. Back to business as usual.) And then Samuel will most likely say something about how many more cars there are around here nowadays. Maybe he'll even tell me again that two of his girls have been riding to the produce auction alone for the last couple months. "I guess her work was done," he might say. "God must have wanted her." Pure. Simple. Plain.

I hope I don't see Samuel for a while, because right now I'd ask him, "Why does it always have to be about work? Screw her *work*. What about her life? What's that worth? Not as much as yours on the Amish hierarchy, right?" Again I feel shame. We all know that horrible things happen and people die inexplicably, and it's not always somebody's fault. I could just as well be going off on the old woman who drove the van that rearended the buggy. (Why aren't I?) Why didn't she turn in her license years ago? Why wasn't she paying attention? Why . . . ? Why am I taking it out on the Amish, who have, after all, lost another one of their own?

I've discovered that what I don't understand about the Swartzentruber life bothers me the most. How could something as small as adding a lantern on a buggy, for instance, create a split in a Swartzentruber church? As I've said, the Swartzentruber Amish are the only Amish I know of to refuse and resist the slow-moving vehicle sign. Some Amish have been fined and even jailed, so the Swartzentruber Amish of Ashland

County reached a compromise with the state. They agreed to seventy-two inches of reflective metal, with sections lining the top, bottom, and sides of a buggy's rear end, in the shape of a box with missing right angles. Samuel's church group also compromised with the state by agreeing to a second lantern light. Now he has one light up high on the driver's side of the buggy—which would be the passenger's side of a car—and one lantern on the opposite side, lower on the buggy.

However, not everybody was willing to accept this compromise. The Swartzentruber Amish family that lives up the road from Samuel is headed by John, Daniel's father, and John's splitting from the church is the reason Daniel and Rebekah could never marry no matter how many pumpkins they toss together. John is a good neighbor to Samuel and a good friend. Their kids go to the same one-room block schoolhouse a couple of miles down the road. But they can't talk about church matters. "He's a good friend," Samuel says, "and a good neighbor. We can talk about anything but church. We just can't talk about the church." Samuel's church group consists of ninety-three families. The group, however, has members in Ohio, Tennessee, and Ontario. Within Samuel's group are districts. For instance, Samuel's church district was determined by how close church group members live to each other, and by how many people can fit in somebody's home for church. All Samuel and Mary's family members belong to Samuel's church group, but the guy living across the street does not. And another Swartzentruber Amish family, about half a mile from John's, belongs to yet another affiliation. John used to be a member of Samuel's church group. But now, even though he lives across the street, he is no longer affiliated with Samuel's church. If you look closely, you'll see minor differences between these two groups. While Samuel's buggy has the two lanterns, John's has only one. John and others of similar disposition split from Samuel's church group and started their own. By refusing to affix the second lantern to the buggy, John's group is breaking Ohio law. They face fines, even jail, if caught.

John is a minister of his church. Ten years ago he went to jail for three days. The environmental arm of the Ashland County Department of Health saw that new Amish houses were being built that were not in compliance with regulations. According to the county's regulations, an outhouse had to be built above a five-hundred-gallon concrete septic tank, not just a hole in the ground. Samuel didn't like it, but he put the tank in when he knew the law was a fait accompli. The county's Amish were furious about the measure, mainly because of the outlay of money but also because the "state" had intruded where it had no right to intrude. The county feared the groundwater from a nearby lake—which provides drinking water for a whole community —would be contaminated. All of the Amish eventually complied. John was the last holdout. He refused the county's mandate and served three days in jail. John is one in a long line of Amish who have been jailed—whether over safety regulations, attending public schools, or refusing to fight in a war—because they would not compromise their beliefs. When he was released, he still had to install the tank, which he did. John sees himself and his church group as even more conservative and traditional than Samuel's group. And when I look closely, I notice that the women of John's church group wear their dresses just a tad lower than the women in Samuel's group, whose dresses are down to their ankles.

⤜ ⤛

The girls and young women always seem to get the worst of it, or at least that's the way it feels today. When an eighteen-year-old guy leaves the Amish, he'll often crash with other guys his age, on the floor or the couch of a buddy. If a girl or young woman does the same thing, she's putting herself in a vulnerable position. She's lived her life with the knowledge that she's a second-class citizen. Among the Swartzentruber Amish, the Ordnung doesn't appear to neglect a thing when it comes to women. Women are not permitted to wear bras or use tampons; they usually use a torn piece of a bedsheet for their menstrual needs. Women cannot use any kind of makeup, perfume, or birth control. They cannot shave their underarms or legs; hair grows where it grows, the way God created it. Nor do women cut their hair. Although cigarettes and chewing tobacco are forbidden, men are allowed to smoke a pipe or a simple cigar. Women are not allowed to smoke at all.

A twenty-year-old ex-Amish woman I spoke with not long ago, who had been out for ten months, recounted stories of encounters with guys that would make anybody's skin crawl. When she found a "boyfriend" who had an apartment, she stayed with him for about a week before she learned he was dealing drugs and had people after him. Although this young woman had convinced herself she loved this guy and he her—after only knowing him for two weeks—she soon discovered the truth. She was startled from her sleep by the guy's hands on her neck, strangling her. She didn't go to the police until he abused her a few more times. Where could she go, anyway? She wouldn't go back to being Amish. She knew almost nobody in the outside world. She was in a devil-you-know situation. When she did finally go to the police, she was told that the guy was no good and that she had to leave him. Living in a much safer place now, she has a new boyfriend. And this one's for real.

God knows, I would not want the Amish life for my daughters. I believe it's too hard, too rigid and restrictive, too highly gendered. Are the women happy? I keep asking myself. I hope I'm not merely patronizing Amish women by asking this. If a man isn't comfortable in the life, he at least has standing and authority. An uncomfortable or unhappy woman has her chores and her children. Her Monday and Friday wash days. Her three-meal-a-day cooking duties. Her eight or ten or twelve pregnancies. And yet I have walked past the Shetler home numerous times in the middle of a summer afternoon with my feet moving to the sound of Mary's whistle. It pierces the day. Her whistle, her smile, her easy laughter, and her love of her family all tell me she is happy, that she loves her life.

She also has a well-developed sense of humor. Barely able to stifle a laugh, she recently told me something Lena had said earlier that morning. Rebekah had been taking antibiotics, but she didn't want to take them that morning because she had skipped breakfast and was afraid her empty stomach would be upset. When Lena heard this she said, "Grandma takes drugs all the time. Is that why she's so upset every day?" Mary laughed hard and long at this retelling. A couple of her daughters overheard and they too laughed. Samuel's stepmother has been rumored to take pain pills and a couple of psychotropic drugs. There's always been a little tension between Mary and Samuel's stepmother. According to Samuel, his stepmother doesn't like Mary much. It's hard to imagine anybody not liking Mary. The old lady might be jealous because Mary has a large and loving family, something she never had.

"But my mom," Samuel says. "My mom was real proud of Mary."

And Mary has a secret life invisible to most outsiders. Mary loves to write letters to her family, and she loves to read. The women are often the ones who write something called circle letters to their siblings. Because Mary has thirteen siblings, when she receives a circle letter, fourteen pages long, one for each sibling's family, she removes her old page of correspondence and writes a new one, letting everybody know what she and the family have been up to since the last circle letter arrived. Because Pennsylvania Dutch is only a spoken language, these letters are written in English, although there may be a greeting in Amish. The circle letters resemble in content the family briefs that appear in the *Budget*. In our area, which is the West Salem area, the scribe is Mrs. Harvey Hostetler. In a recent *Budget* brief she wrote:

> It's a cool morning. We had sunshine and no rain last week I don't think, so people were busy with produce etc. On May 31 it rained very spotty. At some places they had inches of rain in a short time . . . Our church was at Freddie Hostetlers' . . . Herman A. Hostetler, age 42, was ordained minister in Levi Lehman's home district . . . On June 6 was the barn and shed

raising at Abe P. Hershbergers.' On June 6 twenty years ago
was our barn raising, and on the same date 24 years before
that the Weaver barn was put up where Atlee Weavers live
now.

News of births fills out the remainder of the column.

Somehow it comforts me to view the women as the scribes
of Amish life; there is a certain power in that.

Mary also has the hidden life of an insatiable reader. In her
spare time—which is difficult to imagine her having—she reads
books published by Herald Press in Pennsylvania, which are
basically books written by Mennonites or higher-order Amish
for other Amish. One of her favorite authors is a Mennonite
woman who writes under the pen name Carrie Bender. A note
at the beginning of her books reads in part: "Carrie Bender . . .
is a member of an old order group. With her husband and children, she lives among the Amish in Lancaster County, Pennsylvania." Mary reads these books as quickly as she gets them. In
one series, an Amish wife and mother named Miriam writes in
her journal, telling the story of her life through her periodic en-
tries. Despite occasional heartache, things generally turn out
fine for Miriam and her family. A synopsis for Miriam's Journal,
Volume 3, *A Joyous Heart,* reads:

Nate [Miriam's husband] has settled his tax problems, and
now he and Miriam are contentedly raising their children.
Life on the farm is peaceful and rewarding in spite of problems that crop up. Then suddenly illness and death strike the
family. Blaming herself, Miriam finds it nearly impossible to
cope with the grief. On top of that, Miriam and Nate worry

about their good friends, Priscilla and Henry, who seem to be straying beyond the lifestyle approved by their Amish church. Not until Miriam forgives herself and trusts God to redeem the situation does peace and joy fill her heart again.

Some central messages of Amish life are embedded in this synopsis. A tax problem involves Nate's coming clean and paying what the law requires, because even though the Amish are separate from the world they obey the laws not in conflict with their beliefs. Once that problem is solved everything is back to Amish life as it should be—"peaceful and rewarding." And then hardship strikes, as it always does. When Miriam's daughter dies, she blames herself for believing in an unorthodox doctor who ended up being a fraud. By the time they sought the help of conventional medicine, it was too late. Friends of theirs are "straying" from obedience to the church rules, so, of course, Miriam and Nate are worried about them, as they must be. The final message, however, is the one everything else rests on: when Miriam puts her trust in God, peace and joy are restored.

I have to admit that after reading several of these books I could see their appeal for an Amish woman, and maybe for a lot of other people. A strong and good female narrates the books. The very best of Amish life gets represented, and yet clearly the characters are real, and flawed. Pain and suffering often descend on decent people living a good life. And with God on their side, all ends up fine.

I found myself wanting to believe in this world too, a world that unfolds like a story where good people love, suffer, and survive as they act out their roles as characters controlled by a loving narrator.

To live among these people is to be forever conflicted.

It pleases me to no end that Mary has a private, slightly subversive life: the life of a reader, which might have started when she taught school.

If the home and church can be considered masculine—father, deacon, minister, bishop—the school is clearly feminine, although feminine under the direction of the masculine. School is not nearly as important as church and home. Teaching is certainly women's work among the Swartzentruber Amish. Amish teachers, girls and young women often unbaptized and single, receive little training, although they do substitute teach. Pay for a teacher is about eight hundred dollars a year. Boys can make more than that working construction, so the job falls to women. Although you'd never find a woman serving as bishop, minister, or deacon, you'll find one in the front of nearly every Swartzentruber schoolroom.

As linguistic anthropologist and Amish scholar Karen Johnson-Weiner writes:

> Schools are marginal in Swartzentruber life. In part, this may be because none of the children and few of the teachers are baptized, so, although the church community is concerned that the school reflects its values, church members are not involved in school activities. More likely, however, schools remain at the periphery of church-community life, because children learn the important lessons—how to manage the farm and the house or how to care for children—at home, and they gain knowledge one must have to join the church through parental and ministerial introduction . . . Since children do not learn the important lessons in school, a female

teacher, generally underage with no special training and isolated from governing boards that meet infrequently at best, is considered sufficient.

Most Amish will tell you that formal education beyond the eighth grade will only force Amish young people to join English schools, which would expose them to the outside world and could lead to feelings of pride. The other advantage of children leaving school with only an eighth-grade education, of course, is that children who do think of leaving the fold will have to face the prospect of employment in twenty-first century America armed with only a grade-school education. Most often the children who try to leave and then come back to Amish life do so because suddenly they have entered the outside world with a rudimentary education with which to secure a job and no money to go without one.

Obedience, memorization, and learning basic English and math are what's important in a Swartzentruber Amish school. Jonas, for instance, who received As and Bs throughout his eight years of school, probably reads on a second-grade level. Rote learning is more important than critical thinking. The boys learn so many valuable skills around the farm, they're able to make a living farming or working construction, especially if they stay Amish. The boys who leave do so with valuable, marketable skills. Almost all the Amish men I know work well with their hands. They can often get work as carpenters or bricklayers. Employers love Amish employees. They'll work all day long for little pay, and they work hard. An eight-hour day is a light day for an Amish youth.

A girl or young woman who leaves, however, leaves with

skills not as easily marketable. Most ex-Amish girls end up cleaning houses for the English with no benefits or job security.

The Swartzentruber schools of Ashland County are block buildings painted white. They're approximately eight hundred square feet and covered with a tin roof. The Shetler children attend the school two miles from their home. They account for six of the thirty or so students who attend the Albion School. Children from three other families fill out the class. Eighth graders, first graders, and every grade in between are all under the same roof and the tutelage of the same teacher.

Recently I visited the school the Shetler children attend while it was closed for the summer. (I could not get permission to visit the class while school was in session, and I have no doubt the presence of an English man would have affected teacher and students if I had.) "Good Bye and have a good one," was written in English cursive on the blackboard. (The board was literally black, not the green that passes for black in the English schools I've attended.) This school, like all Swartzentruber schools, was built on the land of an Amish farmer. The building is set well back from the road and is surrounded by barbed wire and a metal gate, identical to the gates that lead to Samuel's back pastures. Beneath the blackboard is a twelve-foot-long wooden bench painted gray. The floors are oak. Books, supplies, and sponges used as erasers sit on a shelf above the blackboard. The alphabet is written in cursive above the board as well, upper- and lowercase both represented. Shelves, white and five feet wide, stand against the east wall, from oak floor to wood ceiling. A bottle of Windex, a few small boxes, and rugs for winter foot wiping appear alone on the shelves. A small window is cut into the wall to the west of the blackboard; underneath it are hooks for coats. Next to the shelves hang a thirty-day clock and a calendar. Ironically, the calendar has a picture of a tractor on it—no doubt a freebie from the local feed shop. Two wooden desks in the front of the room face the children—the teacher's desk and a similar one for a substitute or a helper. Each is about three feet wide with two drawers beneath the desktop. A five- or six-inch wood border runs along the front of the desk; the border turns the corner for several inches on each side, which makes the border a bookshelf with bookends. About thirty old-time wood and metal desks common to schoolkids the country over face the teacher in traditional rows. On the wall to the east of the blackboard is a two-and-a-half-foot-long sheet of white lined paper with English cursive writing on it. I see that it's a sample letter, a model to mimic. There's a heading in the top right corner for the sender's address, and then lines for the greeting, body, closing, and signature. This one reads:

Dear Wilma,
We plan to come to your place on Sunday. I will bring my
skates along that I got for Christmas. Lets [sic] hope the pond
is frozen.
Your friend. Becky.

(I have yet to see a Swartzentruber Amish kid with ice skates, and I wonder if this isn't a teacher's hopeful fiction, or perhaps something more suspect and subversive?)

There are twelve-pane windows, nine in all, permitting in a world of natural light. The west wall houses the wood stove and pipe that will heat the school in the winter. The men of the area gather every fall to cut firewood to fill the tin woodshed on the school grounds. The teacher will usually get in early on winter mornings and start a fire in the stove. Boys will carry in wood for the stove during the school day. On the east wall, concrete steps lead to a landing and a gray wooden door; the landing has walls on three sides and is covered by a tin roof. On the south wall of the building there's a hundred-square-foot mudroom with concrete floors, a shelf about four inches up from the floor —for winter boots—and another shelf above rows of hooks. The shelf above the hooks is for hats and bonnets. There's also a shelf beneath the top shelf, leaving just enough space for glasses of water. The mudroom also has a twelve-pane window. I walk out to the first of two outhouses. Yes, it looks like everybody's idea of an outhouse, only a lot cleaner than most I've seen. The first one is a three-seater, with the third seat just a few inches lower than the other two. A roll of toilet paper hangs on each side; one roll is held by wire, the other by a piece of twine stretched from one nail to another a few inches away. Each seat—hole really—has a wooden lid that opens and closes on hinges. All lids are shut for the summer. The other outhouse has only two seats and clearly belongs to the boys. It's identical in all other respects, but it has two seats and a small hole on the front side. And then I see it. From just to the left of the door is a section of white plastic sewer pipe, with the top half removed, placed at an angle, creating a gutter. One end of the pipe rests on a piece of wood between two studs and the end fits into the hole in the front of the seats. Running the length of the pipe and attached to the wall is a piece of vinyl a couple of feet high that acts as a splash guard. An Amish urinal.

On the east end of the schoolhouse roof is a wooden belfry

sheltering a bell, whose peals introduce the beginning of the school day.

One day when Samuel was teaching me how to shuck speltz, I asked Barbara, the third-oldest sibling and daughter, who's pretty, taller than her older sister, and appears to be growing into the big-boned bounty of her mother, what her favorite subject in school was. She answered, "English." Samuel immediately responded with a jocular "ha," and went on to mumble his disapproval of her favorite subject. Barbara has never appeared as content as her sisters, so it's hard not to imagine that she isn't naturally accepting of this life. Was her saying that English was her favorite subject a way of telling her father and me of her discontent? A week or so before, Samuel wondered aloud about what had been getting into Barbara lately. While Rebekah has always wanted to do anything her father did—driving five plow horses through the field at age ten, helping with machinery repair and barn work—Barbara has preferred to stay around her mother, tending to house chores.

"Lately, she's been acting like a five-year-old," he had said of Barbara.

When I heard Samuel say this, I immediately tensed with worry. The Swartzentruber Amish society—like all Amish orders—is a patriarchy. Only men can be bishops, ministers, or deacons. The hierarchy ranges from the oldest baptized men, who have the most authority, to the youngest girls, who have the least, if any. Barbara can be made to do whatever needs to be done. "Rebekah wants to get out and see what she can do," Samuel said. "Barbara is scared to do anything new, but I told her she had to and then she liked it."

Because the man is clearly and officially the head of the

home, the girls are at his mercy. A kind and gentle man like Samuel will be a kind and gentle presence with absolute authority. His polar opposite will possess the same absolute authority and will wield it in his own crude and brutal way. Here's where I have to stop myself and ask if I'd be thinking all of this if I'd heard a non-Amish friend complain that his thirteen-year-old daughter had been acting "like a five-year-old." I doubt if I would have given the statement another thought, even though it could easily be argued that a patina of patriarchy covers us non-Amish modern Americans as well.

After I'd asked Barbara about her favorite subject, I wanted to know if she was going into the eighth grade, her final year of school. Before she could answer, Samuel said, "She better be. Look how big she's getting." Barbara does have the stocky shape of her mother, and I worry how she'll take this comment. She doesn't appear fazed. I honestly believe Samuel did not mean it pejoratively. She's just big, and someone her size is usually out of school or soon will be. Samuel chose Mary as a wife, and Mary has always been heavy. Samuel, as I've said, is thin and fit. Despite the second-class status females hold in the formal structures of Swartzentruber Amish life, one thing seems apparent: Amish girls and young women do not seem plagued by the messages about body image that have led to so many cases of eating disorders among their English counterparts. Without television, movies, and popular magazines, the only women Swartzentruber Amish girls see around here are other Amish girls and the rural women of the county. Indeed, with only their face, arms, and, in summer, their feet visible to the outside world, bodies are not as easily objectified. The clothes worn by

Amish women are designed to signal their separation not from Amish men but rather from the outside world.

Sometimes this insistence on separation from the outside world turns deadly. We English have created an increasingly dangerous world from which the Swartzentruber Amish have chosen to remain apart. But they can't. Not completely. Amish children tucked away in a one-room schoolhouse in Lancaster County, Pennsylvania, were not insulated from a deranged milkman and his murderous modern weapons. The Amish will continue to ride in buggies, kids standing up in back, on roads where cars drive anywhere from fifty to seventy miles an hour. Does this mean they love their children any less than we love ours? I have to wonder about the dangers we've created for our own kids: global warming, watered-down education, war every decade or so. These are not as concrete, however, as a child standing in the back of a buggy. It's hard not to see the buggy fatality as avoidable. It didn't have to happen. Buggies break as easily as kitchen matches. And if you're going to stick with buggies, shouldn't you at least make them big enough to fit a family, so children are not forced to stand up in the rear with nothing but dumb luck between the backs of their heads and the surface of the road?

→ ←

I drove by the home of little eight-year-old Elizabeth just after I learned of the accident. At least fifty buggies packed the area around the house. Men were in the fields, letting a father grieve for his daughter. Women cleaned the house and cooked food, preparing for the funeral. Nobody knew yet if Elizabeth's mother would be released from the hospital in time to bury her daughter.

I stopped at the Shetler farm on my way home. The kids were dressed in clean clothes, having just returned from visiting Elizabeth's family. Andy and Jacob chased each other around the yard, shirttails out and flapping. Rebekah and Barbara talked on the front porch. Samuel was still helping a neighbor thrash speltz, and Mary was inside her home. Clara stood on a ladder painting the window frames of the new house.

Hearing some banging from the buggy shop, I popped in to see if my wheel was painted and ready to go. It was, so I loaded it in my truck. When I got home I stuck it in the wet ground in front of my house, just in front of a desk-size rock with our address stenciled on it, and ran my fingers along the deadly, sacred spokes.

ELEVEN

Another Leaving

The next time I saw Jonas, the first thing I noticed was his hair. He'd dyed it blond. At first glance, he looked like a typical English kid. He wore jeans and an outlandish yellow Cocoa Puffs T-shirt with that bird on it. He also seemed more relaxed around Nora, around Kathleen, even around me. I didn't know how much had happened since we last saw each other.

After two months without a job and still no closer to having his papers, Jonas got a couple of breaks. He was offered a construction job putting up pole barns, by an ex-Amish guy and his wife. Because the boss is ex-Amish, he was willing to hire Jonas off the books. The guy had an arrangement with a pastor near Mansfield, Ohio. The pastor had a house Jonas could share with other ex-Amish, and the rent was reasonable. Jonas would be living and working with three other ex-Swartzentrubers, all of whom had once lived within a couple miles of his boyhood home.

But first he had to move out of the Gilberts' home. Jonas went through a tough time when he was preparing to leave. He and Kathleen argued constantly, and Jonas was often sullen and disagreeable. He also worried about how much he would miss Kathleen's young son, because the two had gotten so close over the year he'd lived there.

His leaving was far more difficult than he'd imagined. "When I left [the Gilbert's home] to work, it felt like I was leaving my family all over again," Jonas said.

Jonas moved to a small run-down house with his three ex-Swartzentruber cohorts. Although the house isn't much, Jonas likes being independent and working every day, and each kid has his own room. They split all the costs evenly, whether it's money to rent a movie or just to pay for utilities. "It's kind of funny. When we were still Amish, we talked to each other some but not much, and now we're living together," Jonas said. He works ten to twelve hours a day, leaving before seven in the morning and not getting home until after eight at night. "We laugh because we talk about what we did when we were Amish. We laugh about the way we'd party on the weekend and that now we don't party at all."

They have a big stereo and speakers they picked up at a yard sale. "We listen to mostly country, but every now and then I listen to rock 'n' roll and different kinds of music," Jonas said. They also have a TV, but they need more dishes for eating. Jonas says he's been having a tough time saving any money. He pays $150 a month to the Gilberts for boarding his horse. "If I can make it, I'll keep the horse, but if I don't have any money left, I'll have to get rid of my horse. It'll be the first thing to go." He hopes he can sell her for $1,500.

When I talked to Jonas after he left the Gilberts' place, I detected a difference in the way he spoke. He told me that he and the other ex-Swartzentrubers spoke Amish in the house, and that he was the only one who wanted to speak English. I soon learned that Jonas still had one foot in the English camp and one in the Amish. He started talking about not needing his GED, and maybe not needing a job that would require him to pay taxes. When another of the ex-Swartzentruber guys he was living with fell off the roof of a house they were working on, Jonas and his other housemates chipped in money to help pay the hospital bills. The hospital kept the kid overnight. Doctors told him he needed to have an operation to have a plate put in his head, but because it would cost too much, the kid decided not to do it. Although they had at first refused, the kid's parents did show up at the hospital the night after he was taken to the emergency room. His mother asked him if he knew why he fell and he said, "Yeah, I didn't have the ladder right," and his mother said, "It was the devil dropping you to see if you still wanted to be English."

Just a month after the boys started living together, one of their fathers died, so the kid went home. According to Jonas, the kid told his family that "he was keeping his cell phone no matter what."

"For all of us who lived there, it seemed to us when he left that he was the one who died," Jonas said. "It just seemed like someone was missing."

→ ←

It soon became apparent that Jonas didn't want to talk about anything depressing on that day. Nora had called me a few days earlier to give me the news: Jonas had gotten his passport and a Social Security card. He was almost home free.

The obstacles in his path had fallen like dominoes. Out of nowhere Jonas got a call from his father's cousin, a guy who had left the Amish eight years before and was now living nearby and working as a bricklayer. He said he'd heard about Jonas leaving and wanted to know if he could do anything to help him. Within days of the call, Jonas had his affidavit, his cousin attesting to the fact that Jonas's father had lived in the States for the years required for Jonas's citizenship. A while later Nora was surfing the Net, looking for help. She landed on the Web page of an English guy from Canada who was living in the States and having some trouble becoming an American citizen. She e-mailed him, but although he was willing to help, there wasn't much he could do because he knew nothing about the Amish. Then a woman who works at the U.S. consulate general in Toronto learned of this guy's website and called him to see if she could help. He told her about Jonas. And then Nora stepped in and things took off.

"I truly believe that there are angels. That God puts angels on earth and when it's time for something to work out, it will work out, and that's what happened to Jonas," Nora said.

To the Swartzentruber Amish of Jonas's church, people who help Amish kids leave are not angels at all. They're people living in the modern world with a grudge against the Amish who get a kick out of corrupting their children.

The woman at the consulate told Nora she needed all of Jonas's paperwork, including his long-form Canadian birth certificate, the affidavit, his school records, his father's birth certificate, and any other thing she could find. Nora and Jonas got the documents together and mailed them to Toronto. A few weeks later, Nora received a call from a woman named Julie at the consulate. She said she'd be able to help if Jonas could get to

Toronto. Nora asked her how Jonas would be allowed to cross the border without photo identification. Julie said she'd send a letter to the border guards, explaining the situation. Nora and Jonas were worried and cynical, but they set out for Toronto on a ninety-degree day in early August 2006, one year and eight months after Jonas left the Amish. On the way there they stopped at a Wal-Mart in Erie, Pennsylvania, so Jonas could get a passport picture taken. As they drove, all Jonas could say was "It ain't going to happen anyway. It ain't going to happen." He'd been close before.

When they finally got to the border and explained the situation to the guard, he asked them to pull up. He needed them to go through a secondary border check. "I was a nervous wreck," Nora recalled. "Jonas was laughing at me."

Julie had arranged for them to get a room near her home, and the night Nora and Jonas arrived she came down to meet them and to look over his documents again. "I have some bad news," she said. Jonas expected the worst. She said she had to be out of the office the next morning, but if they could be there first thing, she might be able to process him then. The next morning Nora and Jonas followed Julie to the consulate, where she gave Jonas a passport application. Nora helped him fill it out, because of Jonas's trouble comprehending and spelling. With that finished, Julie told them that if all went well, Jonas would have his passport the next day.

Jonas and Nora spent the rest of the day in Toronto shopping at the mall, resting, and killing time. When Julie called, she said that the computers were down and so she couldn't find out if the application was being processed. Nora feared that because Jonas had forgotten to pay the passport application fee, the process was being held up. Every complication or obstacle felt like he was taking one more step away from getting his passport.

The next morning they woke up early and went directly to the consulate. Julie was not there to meet them, so they explained to the security guard who they were and that they'd just been there yesterday. He wouldn't let them in until he noticed Jonas's shirt. He had on the same one he had worn the day before: the yellow Cocoa Puffs T-shirt with that bird. He let them in.

When they met Julie upstairs, she said she'd be able to get him a one-year passport, and that it should only take about fifteen minutes. Two hours passed and they had not seen Julie. How would he ever get back into the United States if he didn't have a passport? What if he was turned back at the border? Jonas couldn't understand why Julie and everybody else at the consulate were suddenly preoccupied.

What Jonas didn't realize was that the consulate was in chaos on the morning of August 10 because of the arrest of twenty-four people British authorities believed were part of a plot to blow up ten planes headed to the United States. Jonas waited and waited, growing increasingly frustrated and fatalistic with every minute. After all this time and all he'd been through, he might not even be able to get back into the States. After fleeing his family and his church, entering one life and leaving another, working for a crook and a sex offender, cutting himself off from his parents, relatives, and friends, wondering if he'd ever get his driver's license, realizing just how hard it all was in the wider world, his dream could be derailed once again, this time by something happening on another continent. The wait stretched on and on. No sign of Julie.

And then fifteen minutes after he'd just about given up hope, Julie's assistant came out and told him he'd have his passport shortly. Not ten minutes later, Jonas had proof—for the first time in his life and for the rest of it—that he was an American citizen.

"I just couldn't believe that I got my passport. All that and it's just a little book with my picture on it," Jonas said as he handed me his passport to look at.

"All the way back from Canada we talked," Nora said. "We talked about a lot of serious things, and also funny things."

Before he got his passport, Jonas had said he'd probably just stay with the pole barn guy, but now he was starting to dream again, about an official job with benefits and taxes, about buying a car and getting a place of his own. Samuel has asked me a couple of times if Jonas had his driver's license yet. It seems as if getting the driver's license signals the end of hope for the family of the people who leave. The next time he asks, I'll have to admit that Jonas is now a lot closer to having it and staying gone.

As I drove home from the Gilberts', where Jonas visited almost every weekend, I felt good for Jonas and a little sad for his parents and for Samuel. The only other dark cloud on the day was how angry Jonas was at the church. He blamed his parents not at all; he aimed all his ire at the church. "The way my dad talked to me [at the sawmill three months before, the last time they'd talked] there seemed to be something missing. He doesn't really want me to know that he would have helped me but that the church was putting pressure on him, but I know that's what it was. I just wish my dad wouldn't have to go through all that."

Although Jonas misses spending time with his family, he doesn't appear to have regrets about leaving the Amish. He has more freedom than he would ever have had as a Swartzentruber Amish. He no longer answers to a church or a people. The world is his to travel and explore. But he has given up a few things. He will never be part of a community as tight or as caring as the one he left. He will live as an outsider both among the English and among the Amish he hopes to visit. He has given up a certain identity, and taken on another, less defined, more malleable one. To the English he will always be the Amish kid who crossed over. To the Amish, he will be the one who got away, God help him.

Driving past Samuel's house, I beeped and waved, recalling the last thing Jonas had said earlier that day and how odd and sad it sounded to me, as if Jonas were suddenly aware of something being irretrievably over. "One thing I really miss about being Amish," he said, "is when they'd [Nora and Kathleen] come over and we'd all talk for hours, my dad and everybody. I really miss that."

TWELVE

The World Inside, and Out

About a week before my daughter's wedding, Samuel and Mary invite me into the trailer to show me the wedding gift they've bought her.

"It's hanging right here," Samuel says.

I walk back and see a beautiful thirty-day wall clock, complete with a pendulum, chimes, and Roman numerals. The clock is nearly identical to the one hanging in their makeshift kitchen on another wall of the trailer. A genuine Amish clock. Samuel has had the gift hanging on his wall for a week just to make sure it's keeping good time. "I had to do a little adjusting on ours when we first got it," he says.

My wife and I have invited Samuel and Mary to our daughter's wedding. Although they have not given us an answer yet on whether they will attend the service, they do tell us that the reception is out of the question. Still, Samuel is curious to hear an English sermon.

Although we have had lunches, dinners, and homemade ice cream in the Shetlers' house, they have never accepted an invitation to ours. Just last year around Christmastime we invited the entire family over for some plum pudding. I know they like plum pudding because I have made it for them every year for the last decade. (Either they like it or they're too polite to tell me they don't.) We assured the family that we would have a fire going in the fireplace for heat and use only kerosene lamps when they visited, but still they had to turn us down. Some other Amish who did not have close English friends might have perceived the visit as the Shetlers' attending an English party, complete with sex, drugs, and rock 'n' roll.

The afternoon of my daughter's wedding, amidst all the excitement, the greeting of guests, posing for pictures, trying to make everything perfect, I couldn't help keeping one eye on the church doors for Samuel and Mary.

They didn't come.

But they did ask us over for homemade ice cream and popcorn—two snacks the family is convinced were made to eat together—so they could give our daughter the Amish clock they'd bought her. We arrived around six in the evening, Swartzentruber Amish time, carrying paper plates, brownies, and whipped cream in a can. We sat around the table laughing and talking for the next few hours. Luckily we were there just before dark, which allowed us to experience three kinds of light: daylight, the light of dusk, and then the night's darkness pierced with light from the Shetlers' kerosene lamps. We asked Samuel and Mary about their wedding and they asked me and my wife about ours. The Shetler kids laughed easily, particularly when my wife accidentally squirted a stream of whipped cream on Andy. And soon the kids were squirting each other. Barbara and Rebekah sat on chairs away from the table, since we were taking up their usual spots. Samuel held Esther on his lap. I felt love for every person there that night, as I gazed on the faces of friends lit by the glassed-in glow of a kerosene lamp.

→ ←

A couple of months later, Samuel walked me through his new home, which he hoped to have at a decent stage of completion in a few weeks. The Shetlers were scheduled to have home church then, and there was no way 150 people were going to fit in the trailer. They'd have to do without furniture, but whoever had church two weeks earlier would be bringing the benches.

I'd been in the house probably fifty times since he began building it. I was there when he and a group of Amish relatives and friends knocked down the west wall. I was there when he used a ladder for steps to the upstairs. I even brought over about twenty eight-inch blocks I had lying around, just in case Samuel ended up needing them. (He didn't.) I'm grateful that I was absent the afternoon Rebekah was hit in the face with the chunk of hickory.

Samuel showed me where the kitchen and pantry would be, as well as the front room, the boys' room, and his and Mary's bedroom. He seemed particularly taken with the floor of white and red oak, which he and five friends put down in a couple of days. He finished it off with linseed oil. Varnish is prohibited. It looked beautiful. I've learned that Samuel does not focus much on what he's not allowed to do. He's busy enough doing all he can and all he has to do. We walked upstairs, and he showed me a room with one bed where Rebekah and Barbara will sleep. Rebekah wanted the room in the southwest corner of the house, with windows facing south and west. When we entered a room in the northeast corner, Samuel said to me: "This is the guest room. This is where you'll stay when your electricity goes out."

→ ←

Three weeks later the buggies begin arriving just after eight in the morning, Swartzentruber Amish time. Church will begin at nine. It will be the first church service in the Shetlers' new home. They've been preparing for it for days. Mary, the girls, and Mary's sister have been baking bread and pies, washing windows in the new house, and picking up the stuff around the trailer. Samuel's been in charge of the outside, which included cleaning up wood pieces, sawdust, and other construction debris. The yard and farm look nearly postcard perfect. I drive by several times, counting buggies, listening from the road for words in Old German, peering in windows that I hope will reveal the faces of my friends.

Because even though I have been in the new house fifty-odd times, I will not be allowed in today. Not for church. I continue driving by the house. Today I am nothing but an outsider, an English. For some reason my separateness makes me a little sad. It's the same feeling I get when my wife or kids go on a trip without me, or my dad leaves for a winter in South Carolina, and it's the fear that comes from being apart. My fear rises out of the bleak possibility that I'll never see the person again. It's not rational, of course, especially because I'll probably stop at the farm again tomorrow. Perhaps the source for some of this is the worry I have that this book will injure Samuel and his family in some way. Will he be able to tolerate my ambiguity about his life? Will he be able to forgive my most critical moments? Will he think less of me—and know more of me—when he reads that I would have deeply conflicted feelings about helping his girls leave Amish life if that's what they wanted? Will people in the area who read the book inform other Amish, and will that cause the family church trouble?

Will he have learned too much about the way I feel about the Swartzentruber Amish?

I know I have learned a great deal from the Shetler family and the lives they lead. I've learned that corncobs make great kindling. I've learned the difference between barn swallows and eave swallows. I've learned how to shuck speltz and grind feed. I've learned that some Amish families love with the same love I believe exists in my family and in the family that reared me. I've learned lessons about the bounties and burdens of a close community. I've learned how seriously God's will is trusted. I've learned that some nine-year-old girls have the power to see forever, and that even the plainest of the plain people will do anything to keep their children alive and near them. I've learned that I can drag my sorry heart and weak will to the farm in the middle of a day, and be consoled, completely and utterly, by beliefs I do not or cannot hold. I've learned that I'll never be able to give up listening to music, but that I could give up the next new and improved version of the iPod. I've learned that there are alternatives and values other than those projected by the mass media and our consumer culture. I've learned that perhaps I could live in a post-petroleum age, because I know people who already live that way. I've learned that I need not consume more than I need; and that I should produce my fair share. I've learned to always honor and cherish the land. I've learned that it's important to hold tight to the traditions that are difficult but worthy, and to rid myself of those that perpetuate intolerance of the "other." I've learned that freedom is a relative thing, as are control and conformity. I've learned that at times it's better to contribute to the betterment of a community than it is to seek the upper hand for myself. I've also learned that on one level it's impossible for the individual to be subsumed by the community, yet on another level it's incredibly easy to disappear into ideology or fanaticism. I've learned that leaving one life and entering another is even braver than I'd thought. I've learned that if someone wanted to take their land and their homes, these people I've come to know would simply move away and give it all up rather than defend it by force.

Despite how conflicted I am about aspects of the Swartzentruber Amish way of life, I can still recognize beauty and truth when I see it. And the beauty and truth of it is this: That to these plain people, in these times and in all others, the values that reign supreme are community, acceptance, and faith, which can, with prayer and a little luck, lead to peace.

EPILOGUE

The Shetlers are now in their new home, and it's as beautiful as it is simple.

Hank the dog got his leg run over by a car when he was sleeping in the driveway. The driver of the car, somebody who'd come to buy produce, did not stop, nor has he come back. Hank spent a couple of weeks living under the trailer, being fed and watered by the kids and given Tylenol by Samuel, who had to crawl beneath the trailer to nurse him. Hank's much better now, but he has to get by on only three legs; the fourth hangs uselessly at his side as he runs through the fields.

And no, Samuel did not take Hank to the vet. That's not his way. But he also did not take himself to the hospital when he lost nearly an inch of his right index finger to a thresher blade a few weeks ago. He said it didn't hurt at the time, "but once the nerves found out something was missing, they started pumping like crazy." Mary was too disturbed by his injury to clean and bandage what was left of her husband's finger, so Rebekah did it. And after lunch, Samuel went back to work on the thresher, never checking around for his missing piece. "The only time it hurts is when I forget about it and bump it up against something."

Mary is living the life she lives, the one I believe she's chosen, the one she loves; and this is true for her children, as far as I can tell.

Jonas passed his driving test and now has his license. He almost bought an old Firebird from his boss for a thousand dollars. "It's got wide tires like the car on *The Dukes of Hazzard*," he told me. He settled for a cheap pickup truck instead. And he vows never to return to Amish life, but with his truck he did deliver a load of manure to his father, which the man accepted. "It would be a lot harder to go back to being Amish than it was to leave. I never thought that would be true, but now I know it is."

Samuel is beginning to wonder if perhaps Mary wouldn't consider moving south, to Tennessee maybe, where they have family and where the winters are milder.

And I'm still waiting for Samuel to read this book, and then for us to sit down and have a good long talk, the way friends do.

ACKNOWLEDGMENTS

I'd like first and foremost to thank the Shetler family, not only for making this book possible, but because of their basic goodness. I'm honored to have them as friends.

Thanks to Dr. Donald Kraybill for his amazing generosity, and for all his good work. I'd like to give special thanks to Donald Kraybill for letting an amateur into the fold, and for turning me on to baked oatmeal. I'd also like to thank Dr. Karen Johnson-Weiner, a generous and learned spirit.

Thanks also to Roseann Wagner, Peter Hostetler, and Patricia Ambers.

Thanks go to Joe Keim.

As I often am, I am indebted to my good friend and second reader Dan Lehman, and to Barbara Lehman—"Long live the covering!"

A big thanks to my folks, Jim and Peggie Mackall, who have bugged me for a decade to write this book, and who would have been upset if I hadn't. Thanks also to Bryan and Ann McCarthy, Mary Ogle, and Steve Mackall, family of the highest order. Although they've done nothing to help with this book except for just being who they are, thanks to Jen and Dave Hendren, Katy Mackall, and Dan Mackall. I love you all.

Thanks to my first reader, best friend, and favorite writer, to whom this book is dedicated, my wife, Dandi Daley Mackall.

I am indebted to Ashland University for granting me a semester-long leave in which to begin researching and writing this book. Special thanks to Mike Hupfer and Dr. John Bee for their constant support and to Russell Weaver for his friendship.

Thanks to the exquisite folks at Beacon Press, especially to Helene Atwan for wanting this book, and to Amy Caldwell, a great person and an equally great editor. Also at Beacon, I'd like to thank Tom Hallock, Tracy Ahlquist, and Bob Kosturko. And thanks to Rosalie Wieder for her splendid copyediting.

INTRODUCTION

The Swartzentruber Amish are widely recognized by scholars as the most traditional and conservative of all Amish orders; although less widely known, the Nebraska Amish are viewed by some as being as traditional and conservative as the Swartzentrubers.

Amish population estimates throughout the book are based on several sources, including John A. Hostetler's *Amish Society*; Donald B. Kraybill's *The Riddle of Amish Culture*; Steven M. Nolt's *A History of the Amish*; the work of David Luthy, specifically the 1998 article "The Origins and Growth of the Swartzentruber Amish" (*Family Life*, vol. 31); and firsthand Amish sources.

Information on what is and is not permitted among the Swartzentruber Amish comes from my own extensive interviews with the Swartzentruber Amish of Ashland County, Ohio, and from Donald B. Kraybill and Marc A. Olshan's *The Amish Struggle with Modernity*.

The quote from historian Will Durant appeared in the November 9, 1981, *New York Times* story "Historian Will Durant Dies."

ONE   POP CANS AND DOOMED PIGS

Anyone interested in learning more about the history of the Anabaptists in general and the Amish in particular should begin by consulting the books of Hostetler, Nolt, and Kraybill.

Although a great many Anabaptists refer to what women wear beneath the bonnet as a *covering*, the Swartzentruber Amish of my area call it a *cap*.

The quote on community and salvation by John A. Hostetler is from his book *Amish Society.*

Information on the number of Swartzentruber men who still work on the farm comes from personal interviews and from Kraybill and Olshan's *The Amish Struggle with Modernity.*

Information on the origins of Ohio's Lodi settlement comes from personal interviews.

The 2000 U.S. Census provided the statistics for the population growth of Ashland County, Ohio.

TWO THE LEAVING

All information in this chapter—except for retention statistics—comes from my personal interviews with Jonas, the Gilbert family, and Samuel Shetler.

Information on Amish retention comes from Kraybill and Olshan's *The Amish Struggle with Modernity.*

THREE REMEMBERING SARAH

All information on the specifics of Swartzentruber dress comes from my own personal interviews.

Although research on interaffiliation marriages can be found in a variety of works of Amish scholarship, the information regarding the specific split in Samuel's affiliation and its consequences comes from personal interviews.

Donald Kraybill told me the chiropractor joke on a cold January morning over baked oatmeal in a Pennsylvania restaurant.

All the information on Swartzentruber funerals and their aftermath comes from personal observation and interviews.

FOUR "YOU BE CAREFUL OUT AMONG THEM ENGLISH."

Everything in this chapter comes from my own interviews.

FIVE THE MIDNIGHT TABLE

The Wendell Berry quotes in this chapter appear in his book *The Unsettling of America.*

The specific information on Amish children and their obedience to their parents comes from personal interviews.

All information on Swartzentruber weddings and dating practices comes from personal interviews. Even among varied affiliations of the same order there can be considerable differences when it comes to customs and rituals, and even greater differences between orders.

The story of Tobiah and Sarah can be found in *The New American Bible,* Saint Joseph edition. The story does not appear in generally accepted versions of the Bible.

SIX UNDERGROUND RAILROAD

Information on the Mission to Amish People (MAP) comes from interviews with its founder, Joe Keim, as well as the organization's literature.

The visit Nora Gilbert and Jonas made to his home was recounted to me first by Nora and then by Jonas a while later. I was not there to witness that episode.

SEVEN THE LOT FALLS

All information on the selection and roles of bishops, ministers, and deacons in Samuel's affiliation comes from personal interviews. Some of it is also true for "higher churches" (less conservative orders). And yet each affiliation or order may have its own way of doing things.

The quote from John A. Hostetler is from his book *Amish Society.*

Hostetler's *Amish Society* also provided the version of the Schleitheim Articles used in this chapter.

EIGHT THE AMISH FBI

All information in this chapter comes from personal interviews.

NINE TIME AND SPACE

The Kraybill quote about buggies can be found in *The Riddle of Amish Culture.*

Information on the differences in buggies, household appliances, furniture, and farm machinery among the various orders of Ohio Amish comes from Kraybill and Olshan's *The Amish Struggle with Modernity,* as well as my own interviews with Swartzentruber Amish.

Information on the specifications of Swartzentruber Amish buggies comes from interviews with a local Swartzentruber buggy maker.

For more information on the Supreme Court's ruling in *Wisconsin v. Yoder* (1972), begin by consulting the book *The Amish and the State*, edited by Kraybill.

Buggy accident statistics for Ohio were obtained from the Ohio Department of Public Safety.

TEN **DEADLY SACRED**
Details of the buggy fatality in this chapter were obtained through personal interviews and from the news stories published in the *Ashland Times-Gazette*.

Specifics of the Swartzentruber Ordnung regarding women were learned through personal interviews.

Information on the school the Shetler children attend as well as other Swartzentruber Amish schools in Ashland County was obtained through personal interviews and observation. Information on Swartzentruber schools mostly comes from "The Swartzentruber Schools" by Karen Johnson-Weiner, which appears in the book *Train Up a Child: Old Order Amish and Mennonite Schools*, published by the Johns Hopkins University Press in 2007.

ELEVEN **ANOTHER LEAVING**
All information in this chapter comes from personal interviews.

TWELVE **THE WORLD INSIDE, AND OUT**
All information in this chapter comes from personal interviews and observation.

All Bible quotes are from the King James Version.